To Jess

MW01294449

Thanks for your support!

Best Wishes

[signature]

1-31-16

To Jesse Zuniga

MUSTANG MIRACLE

Humberto G. Garcia

Based on the true story of the San Felipe Mustangs Golf Team, which overcame overwhelming obstacles to win the 1957 Texas State High School Golf Championship.

authorHOUSE®

AuthorHouse™
1663 Liberty Drive
Bloomington, IN 47403
www.authorhouse.com
Phone: 1-800-839-8640

© *2012 Humberto G. Garcia. All rights reserved*

No part of this book may be reproduced, stored in a retrieval system, or transmitted by any means without the written permission of the author.

Published by AuthorHouse 9/18/2012

ISBN: 978-1-4772-6989-3 (sc)
ISBN: 978-1-4772-6988-6 (hc)
ISBN: 978-1-4772-6990-9 (e)

Library of Congress Control Number: 2012917361

This book is printed on acid-free paper.

Certain stock imagery © Thinkstock.

Because of the dynamic nature of the Internet, any Web addresses or links contained in this book may have changed since publication and may no longer be valid. The views expressed in this work are solely those of the author and do not necessarily reflect the views of the publisher, and the publisher hereby disclaims any responsibility for them.

This book is dedicated to the memories of
J. B. Pena and Hiram Valdes,
who made it possible for a group of young caddies
to play golf and become champions.
It is also dedicated to all those who keep the spirit of
San Felipe alive.

FOREWORD

I WAS SITTING NEXT to my teammates at the San Felipe Ex-Students Memorial Center, lamenting the fact that one more putt made by either one of us would have allowed us to avoid losing on a card playoff, when they began announcing the winners of the 2008 San Felipe Ex-Students Reunion Tournament. We certainly had plenty of opportunities to get that one more birdie that would have made us the winners, but we faltered. My friend and teammate, Ramiro Salazar, pointed out that our failure to secure the birdie on the number one handicap hole was about to do us in.

Before the tournament chairman announced us as the second-place team, he mentioned that he wanted to introduce the five members of the 1957 San Felipe High School Golf Team, which won the state golf championship. The four of us making up the team of the 1972 class looked at each other in silent amazement, and another teammate, Rocky Valdes, asked, "Did you guys hear that? Did any of you know about this?"

None of us could give an affirmative response before Rocky continued, "Do you realize how awesome that is for a team from San Fe to win a state championship?"

I didn't answer this rhetorical question, but I added my own question, "Can you imagine the obstacles they faced back then and the odds against them?"

"That has to be one of the most amazing accomplishments I've heard of," chimed in Doctor Rodolfo Urby, another teammate, "but why don't more people know about them?"

"I don't know," I replied, "but I'm going to change that!" I didn't know just then what exactly I was going to do. All I knew was that I had to find a way to tell their story. My mind began racing with ideas on how to begin. I determined that I needed to interview each of the team members to get details about their experience.

Over the course of the next year, I began my research and specifically interviewed the members of the 1957 state championship team, Joe Trevino, Felipe Romero, Mario Lomas, and Gene Vasquez.

To appreciate how amazing their story is, you need to know something about three subjects: San Felipe, the game of golf, and Mexican Americans in the 1950s.

San Felipe refers to the San Felipe Independent School District in the city of Del Rio, Texas, a community located on the southwest Texas-Mexico border. The school district was a product of segregation in Texas, as was common throughout the southern part of the United States where minorities made up a significant part of the citizenry. In the 1950s, the Mexican Americans outnumbered the Anglo population in the border cities, but for years they were subjugated by white rule. Everyone living south of San Felipe Creek, which dissected the city, was deemed a resident of San Felipe and had to attend its schools. Everyone living north of the creek was fortunate to attend the Del Rio Independent School District schools. I say fortunate because even though those in power espoused the principle of "separate but equal," in reality, nothing about the schools in Del Rio prior to 1971 was consistent with that principle. The Del Rio side had better-funded schools and teachers because it had, as its primary source of funding, the money from the federal government that was paid to the district for each student living at Laughlin Air Force Base who attended its schools, even though the base was situated within the San Felipe district boundaries.

San Felipe was created in 1929 out of necessity, that is, because the Del Rio side of the city was not providing and would not provide its Mexican American children with the benefits of a decent education. As a result, 99 percent of the students in San Felipe were Mexican American. The other 1 percent consisted of African Americans, with the occasional Anglo student who either didn't care or didn't know he was receiving an underfunded education. While it was underfunded, the education was not necessarily inferior. In many ways, because the resources were limited, the teachers tended to give more of themselves, even if their devotion and dedication did not entirely make up for what the students were missing in the way of resources.

Of interesting significance to our story is that each school district had its own high school, which led to a well-established and long-standing rivalry. Regardless of the sport, be it football, baseball, or basketball, each side considered it a major victory to defeat the other, even if the team had not beaten any other school during any given season. If a team beat its crosstown rivals, it was considered a winning season. Tensions between the Mustangs from San Felipe and the Wildcats from Del Rio would always rise near game time.

San Felipe existed until 1971. During the summer of 1971, Judge William Wayne Justice of the U.S. District Court for the Eastern District of Texas, sitting at Tyler, Texas, decided to end the segregation. Instead of forcing the Laughlin kids to attend the San Felipe schools, as the lawyers for San Felipe requested, he ordered the two school districts consolidated into one. This marked the end of the San Felipe Independent School District, but it did not end the Mustang spirit nor the loyalty to the purple and gold, the colors that symbolized an era of isolation and segregation to all those who were fortunate enough to attend and graduate from good ole "San Fe."

Now comes the game of golf. If you're not familiar with the sport, you should know that it is a very difficult game to play. If you are familiar with it, then you already know what a challenge it presents. Even today with all of the technological improvements in the implements, it can be extremely trying of your skill and patience. You can hit a good shot but then follow it with ten bad ones before seeing another good one. You can have a great round today and play your worst round ever tomorrow. Why anyone would want to play the game mystifies even the greatest of players, but if you do play, you will not want to stop, no matter how many bad shots you hit. The game presents a challenge that is so addicting that once you finish a round of eighteen holes, you are already making plans for the next one.

The game requires that you hit a stationary ball about one-third the size of a baseball with the head of a club that's about half the size of half a dollar bill and moving at a speed of eighty to one hundred miles per hour.

Lest I forget, you have to hit it straight on an intended target line as far as you can, just so that you can walk or ride toward it to hit it again, and again, until you get it in a hole in the ground about the size of a soup can. Once you have done it a single time, you have to do it seventeen more times over the course of four to five hours. It takes the majority of golfers today over one hundred hits, or strokes of the ball, to accomplish this task. The good players take an average of seventy-five to ninety strokes, while the best players take about sixty-five to seventy-four strokes. Occasionally, you will see rounds of fifty-nine to sixty-four strokes. These are not as common, but they are wonderful to see, especially in professional competitions.

You should keep in mind that the clubs used today are designed so that they are forgiving, that is, they minimize the effects of a poor strike of the ball so that you do not spend most of your round looking for recalcitrant balls that choose to go hide and prevent you from striking at them again. In 1957 and the years before then, there were no such things as forgiving golf clubs. Unless you struck the golf ball perfectly with the "sweet spot" of the club face, a spot the size of a dime, you could expect the ball to take unwanted flight paths, assuming you even got it airborne. With such a small sweet spot, a golfer would have to use his utmost skill to generate the desired trajectory and distance. If golfers played the game today with the clubs available then, undoubtedly, most of them would hardly ever score less than one hundred in a given round. There is only one rational explanation for the golfer of the 1950s to score in the seventies and even sixties in a round—pure, unmitigated skill.

The third essential subject is Mexican Americans. Mexican Americans in the 1950s occupied no better stature in American society than did African Americans. Even though we made up the majority of the population of the border cities, that is, those cities situated on the border with the Mexico, we were considered "different" and unworthy of socializing with the white population. We were not allowed in many restaurants, hotels, and other service establishments. In fact, we were not even allowed to enter the many buildings we helped build. Mexican Americans were certainly not allowed to join country clubs and partake of the game of golf as members. You could have been a billionaire in that time period, but if you were a Mexican American, not even the money could buy you a membership anywhere in the South, especially in Texas. You could work as a greenskeeper or cook or be a caddy for the members, but the doors to membership were solidly shut.

This is the story of four young Mexican American golfers who succeeded despite the obstacles and challenges posed by an unfriendly era in American history.

CHAPTER ONE

It was the summer of 1953, and opportunities to remain occupied in nonschool activities were minimal at best. For young Mexican American boys in the border city of Del Rio, they were practically nonexistent, except for what thirteen-year-old Felipe Romero was about to be introduced to. He had just arrived at his friend Manuel's house to see if Manuel could join him at play, but when he walked up to the door he found Manuel ready to leave.

"Where are you going, Manuel?" Felipe asked. "To the country club," he replied.

"What's that?"

"It's where they play golf. I'm gonna do some caddying," he explained. "You need to come too. We can make some money!"

Now this caught Felipe's attention. He had no idea what Manuel was talking about, but he knew he had to go with him. "Okay, but I have to ask my mom first!"

With that they both ran to the Romero home two blocks away. When they ran in, Felipe found his mother in the kitchen and proceeded to ask for permission. *"Mama, puedo ir con Manuel?"* he asked.

"A donde mijo?" she inquired.

Felipe turned to Manuel, who was standing next to him, and asked, "Where are we going?"

Manuel was caught off guard for a second but then stated, "The country club. Tell her we're gonna make some money!"

"Al country club a ganar dinero, mama!" he said convincingly to his mother.

"Bien pero tengan cuidado!" his mother admonished as she gave her consent. She didn't know what a country club was either, but as long as her son wasn't going someplace where he would get in trouble, she was okay with granting him permission to join Manuel.

Before she could finish her sentence, Felipe and Manuel were out the door and headed to the San Felipe Country Club.

Felipe, a short, skinny, dark-haired son of a typical poor but hardworking father and mother of Mexican descent, had a strong urge to be constantly active. Everyone said that was the reason he was so slim. He seemed dwarfed by Manuel, who was only two years older but tall and quite muscular.

"Come on, Felipe. We've got to hurry before the golfers begin to get there!" Manuel urged.

"But what is it that we're gonna do?" Felipe wondered out loud as the two ran briskly through the streets of South Del Rio, the part of town known as San Felipe.

"I told you we're gonna work as caddies and make some money!" he answered.

"What are 'caddies'?" Felipe asked in between hard breaths while running alongside Manuel.

"We carry the golfers' bags with the clubs, and they give us money," Manuel stated, trying to be patient with Felipe.

"Oh!" Felipe said, seemingly satisfied with Manuel's explanation. But as they continued running along the dirt streets of San Felipe, his inquiry continued. "But what's a golfer?" he asked.

Manuel could not help but stop running and almost wanted to start laughing but held himself back. "You never heard of golf?" he asked in amazement.

Felipe did not want to admit his ignorance of the game but quickly forced himself to do so. "No!" he sheepishly admitted.

Manuel was so understanding for all his fifteen years of life, and he did not want to make Felipe feel bad. "That's okay," he said. "I'll teach you what you need to know, and you'll like being a caddy."

They continued running toward their destination, passing along San Felipe Creek, the unofficial dividing line between white and brown Del Rio.

Like most other country clubs, San Felipe Country Club centered its social activities around a golf course, but it had only nine holes, whereas many have eighteen. It was situated on several acres of public land owned by the City of Del Rio. The irony of its existence was that, although on publicly owned land, at one time the majority of the city's taxpaying citizens could not benefit from it. Several local businessmen had gotten together with the city politicians and arranged for the club to lease the land from the city for one dollar a year for one hundred years. To add insult to injury, the club was allowed to use all the water it needed for its grasses without having to pay for it. Smack in the middle of the course grounds was the San Felipe Springs, the main source of drinking water for the city's entire population.

When they arrived at the course parking lot, other boys longing for the limited work were already there. Some said "hello" to Manuel, while others were reserved; perhaps they thought he was about to take a job away from them.

"*Y este?*" one asked Manuel, pointing to Felipe.

"This is my friend, Felipe," Manuel answered. "I'm going to teach him to be a caddy!"

The boy looked at Felipe again but said nothing and walked away.

No sooner had they gotten there than a brand-new Buick Roadmaster drove up to the parking lot. All of the boys, about twelve in all, rushed over to the driver's side door. As soon as the well-dressed white man opened the door, all of the boys queried him in unison, "Need a caddy, mister? Need a caddy, mister?"

The man did not say anything, but he noticed Felipe, who had worked his way close to the trunk of the car, where the man had moved to.

"Need a caddy, mister?" Felipe meekly asked.

The man smiled and commented, "You don't look older than ten to me, son! How much do you weigh?" he asked.

"I don't know, sir, but I'm twelve!" Felipe proudly pronounced.

"Hell, son, my golf bag weighs more than you! Why don't you come back when you're older and heavier?" As he unintentionally disappointed Felipe, he turned to Manuel and recognized him from previous stints. "You're Manuel, right?" he asked.

Manuel quickly stepped up to him and answered, "Yessir!" He too recognized the man as Ken Johnson, an athletically built, tall man who was well known for his golfing skills.

As the man opened the trunk, he issued instructions to Manuel. "Get my bag, son, and come with me!"

Manuel obeyed and quickly retrieved the golf bag from the trunk. He turned to Felipe and signaled for him to go with him. He then asked the man, while pointing to Felipe, "Can he come with us, Mr. Johnson? I'm teaching him to be a caddy!"

The man paused for a moment, looking at Felipe, and then said, "Yeah, but I'm not paying him!" He didn't wait for any reaction or further requests from Manuel and began walking toward the clubhouse as the two boys eagerly followed. When they got close to the clubhouse, they received additional instructions from the man. "You boys wait right here for me. I'll be back in a bit." He then walked into the members-only building.

Manuel understood why they had to wait outside, for no caddy was allowed to enter the clubhouse, but Felipe was somewhat puzzled. "What's in there?" he asked Manuel.

"I don't know, but we can't go in there. It's for members only," he replied. "When he comes back, he's gonna play golf, and I'm going to carry this bag for him. That's what caddies do. I'll give you a chance to carry the bag for a few holes to get the idea," Manuel said as he began his teaching of Felipe.

"Oh, okay! I can do that!" Felipe confidently asserted.

"You watch me and do what I say," Manuel told Felipe as his lessons began. "You see this?" he asked, pointing to one of the clubs with a dark piece of wood and a red painted square with four screws driven into it. "This is the driver. It's to hit the ball the farthest." He pulled another club from the bag with a piece of dark silver metal with grooves cut along its face in parallel lines. "And this is an iron," he said. "You use it when you don't want to hit the ball as far. This is a putter," he said, pointing to another club with a long and flat piece of shiny metal. "It's used to get the ball in the hole when you get to the green."

"What hole?" Felipe asked.

"Out there," Manuel said, pointing in the direction of the course. "You'll see. Just do what I say and you'll learn! Okay?"

"Okay, Manuel. I will," Felipe responded.

Manuel then opened one of the pockets of the golf bag and pulled out some round white spheres. "These are golf balls," Manuel said, continuing his instructions. "They hit these to try to get them in the holes. You need to watch very closely when Mr. Johnson and the others hit a golf ball 'cause we're gonna have to find it so that they can hit it again until it goes in the hole." As he finished these instructions, Mr. Johnson came out of the clubhouse and walked over to them.

"Let's go, Manuel! We're on the tee box!" he ordered.

Manuel picked up the golf bag and began walking rapidly behind the golfer as he motioned to Felipe to follow. He turned to Felipe and admonished, "Oh, by the way, you need to stay very quiet when they're hitting the ball. If you mess them up, they will never let you caddy for them, okay?"

Felipe nodded affirmatively but said nothing. Now in addition to being confused, Felipe was somewhat scared. The last thing he wanted to do was to disappoint Manuel and lose the chance to learn to caddy. While he did not fully understand everything he had heard from Manuel, he began feeling confident that this was something he could do. He enthusiastically followed Manuel, who moved quickly with Mr. Johnson's bag on his shoulder toward the area where play usually began.

When they arrived at the first tee box, there were three other caddies waiting with their golfers. They were all experienced caddies who regularly worked for the golfers, who had chosen them from among all the eager boys looking for the only work they knew available to them. It was not difficult work, but some people equated the caddies with pack mules who took orders from pushy white men that played a silly game. Those voicing these views simply did not understand the game, and, more importantly, ignored the fact that the boys were doing something honest and productive while they stayed out of trouble.

The first hole was a par three about 135 yards from the tee box to the green. It required the player to hit the ball so that it flew over the San Felipe Creek and up a hill to get to the green where the flag was seen. Mr. Johnson stood at the tee box making some comments to the other golfers that Manuel and Felipe could not hear. He then turned and looked at Felipe and said, "Hey, kid, hand me the niblick, will ya?" Felipe tried hard not to look like he did not know what he had just asked for, but Manuel came quickly to his rescue. He pointed Felipe to the nine-iron in the bag. "The golf club with the nine on it," he whispered, and Felipe reached for it, pulled it out of the bag, and handed it to Mr. Johnson. Mr. Johnson smiled at him and gave him a wink, showing his approval. Manuel nodded his head to say "good going" to Felipe, thus giving him the satisfaction that he was on the way to learning how to become a good caddy. Mr. Johnson proceeded to place the ball on a tee on the ground while everyone remained quiet. He then took his swing and struck, making it fly high and straight in the direction of the green situated on top of the hill across the creek, landing about ten feet from the flag placed in the hole.

"Good shot, Ken!" one of the other players commented.

"Thanks," Mr. Johnson replied as he gave the club back to Felipe. Felipe grabbed it and instinctively knew that it had to be returned to the bag it had come from. He slipped it into the slot he had pulled it from and waited for the other players to hit their shots. As soon as they did, each caddy grabbed his golfer's bag and began walking to the first green. Manuel told Felipe to pick up Mr. Johnson's bag and carry it like the other caddies. He then looked at the first caddy and said, "Hey, Mario, this is Felipe. Felipe, this is Mario Lomas."

"Hi, Mario," Felipe said.

"*Que tal, Felipe!*" Mario greeted.

"This is Joe Trevino," Manuel said, pointing to the other caddy walking along his side.

"Hey!" Joe said.

"Hi, Joe!" Felipe said.

"You caddied before, Felipe?" Joe asked.

Felipe shook his head from side to side and said, "No, this is my first time."

"You'll do okay," Joe said confidently. "Just listen to Manuel. He can teach you a lot!"

"I will," Felipe replied with a smile.

"The other kid over there is Julio," Joe continued. "He's being doin' this for a year. We've been doin' it for three years. We also play. Do you play?"

"Play what?" Felipe answered.

"Golf," Joe said matter-of-factly. "Do you play golf?"

"No," Felipe responded. "But I could do this!" he said with an air of confidence as he struggled to maintain the leather strap of the golf bag on his shoulder while walking behind Manuel.

"Okay. When we get done here, I'll show you how to hit it. You can learn real good from me!" Joe professed as he arrived at the first green.

"You can learn to be as good as Mario there," he said, pointing to the other caddy Felipe had just met. "But you can't be as good as me!" He quickly started laughing and walked toward his golfer.

His was not a false bravado. Before his family had moved from San Angelo to Del Rio in the preceding year, Joe had learned to caddy at a golf course in that city located to the northwest. By the time he started caddying at San Felipe, the tall slender, dark-haired fourteen-year-old had also learned to play the game quite well. He had grooved a good swing, even though he could only hit balls in the practice range when he and the other boys could sneak on while the members gathered inside the clubhouse. While only a year older than Felipe, Joe had developed a mature street sense, having spent his early years in the tough streets of the larger city, and this fueled his self-confidence.

Felipe stared in amazement but said nothing until Manuel got close to him. "Is he a good golfer?" he asked Manuel about Joe.

"Oh yeah!" Manuel answered affirmatively. "You'll see!" He pulled the putter from the bag and gave it to Mr. Johnson, who was studying the green.

"What do you think this putt is going to do, Manuel?" Mr. Johnson asked.

Manuel squatted down and looked at the ground between the ball and the hole. He then got up and walked to the opposite side and squatted down again and gazed at the flag and the area around it. "It's gonna move right about that much," he said confidently as he showed him with his thumb and forefinger a distance of about three inches.

Mr. Johnson squatted down and looked at the same ground. "I think you're right," he said as he stood next to the ball and got ready to make the stroke. He gently pulled the putter back and then forward gently, striking the ball. The ball rolled toward the hole while Felipe paid close attention to its movement. He saw the ball take a slight turn to the right and then disappear into the hole. "Yes!" Mr. Johnson exclaimed as the ball went in.

"Good birdie!" the other golfers said in unison. "Thanks!" he replied as he walked off the green.

"How did the ball do that?" Felipe asked Manuel.

Manuel smiled and simply said, "It just followed the grain and the ground."

"But how did you know the ball was gonna move like that?" Felipe asked.

"The ball moved that way 'cause the green has places that are higher than others and the grass is growing that way," he began to explain while pointing his hand to the right.

"What way?" Felipe asked with a puzzled look.

Manuel smiled and said, "I'll show you when we finish. We gotta move to the next tee right now! C'mon." He walked briskly to the next tee where the golfers were headed.

"Okay," Felipe said with resigned patience. He then moved quickly to the second tee box and waited for Mr. Johnson to ask for a club so he could try to learn more about which clubs were used in different situations. Before Mr. Johnson said anything, Manuel had already pulled a four-iron and was handing it to him. Mr. Johnson said nothing when he grabbed the club and began his pre-shot routine. He knew Manuel had picked out the right club without having to say anything. That's the kind of confidence he had in Manuel. Felipe picked up on this and made a mental note that he would one day be as good as Manuel and instill this same type of confidence in the players for whom he caddied.

Mr. Johnson proceeded to strike the ball down the short fairway and didn't wait for the ball to land before turning to Manuel to hand him the club. The next player to go to the tee box was the player for whom Julio was caddying. He was Dr. Bender, an older gentleman who did not possess nearly the same talent as Mr. Johnson. He asked Julio for a four-wood, which caused Julio to question the selection.

"Doctor Bender, why don't you hit the three-iron 'cause you hook the four-wood too much?"

"I know, but I won't hook it this time. I think I figured it out," the doctor replied. "Let me have the four!"

"Yessir!" Julio meekly replied and handed him the four-wood. Dr. Bender set up his shot, made a few practice swings, and then hit the golf ball with a pronounced right to left flight, causing it to land in the creek that was located to the left of the second hole's fairway.

"Damn!" the doctor exclaimed. He dropped the club by Julio's feet and started walking briskly away from the tee toward the fairway.

"Wait up, Doc!" Mr. Johnson shouted. "Paul and Gregg still have to hit!"

Dr. Bender looked back and mumbled something and then walked to the right away from the line of fire. The other two players hit their shots, and the entire group then walked down the fairway to approach the balls they had hit from the tee. Dr. Bender walked toward the edge of the creek about 150 yards down the fairway as Julio moved quickly toward him.

"Is this about right? Dr. Bender asked Mr. Johnson, wanting to determine where he should drop his ball to make the next shot.

"Yeah, that's fine," Mr. Johnson replied.

Julio pulled a golf ball from Dr. Bender's bag and handed it to him. Dr. Bender then dropped it behind his left shoulder and asked, "What's my distance?"

Julio looked around for several landmarks and then glanced at the little notebook he was carrying.

"You got about 75 yards to lay up so you can hit a wedge over the water and get to the green," said Julio, knowing the doctor was not likely to reach the green from where the ball lay.

"What's the yardage to the green?" the doctor asked.

Reluctantly, Julio responded, "It's 178 to the front of the green, 186 to the pin."

"Give me my four-iron!" the doctor ordered.

Julio took a deep breath and sighed as he handed him the four-iron, which he knew the doctor could not hit well enough to get the ball there. Dr. Bender set himself up and took a wicked swing at the ball in an effort to get to the green but almost missed it entirely. Instead of flying toward its intended destination, the ball trickled into the waters of San Felipe Creek.

"Give me another ball!" he barked at Julio, and Julio quickly complied. The doctor dropped it and attempted to hit it again but with the same result. Julio had already pulled another golf ball from the bag by then, and he gave it to him. This time the doctor made better contact, but the ball shot straight down toward the water. Without skipping a beat, he flung the four-iron in the creek before Julio had a chance to say anything to try to convince him not to take out his frustration on the equipment as he had done many times in the past. Before he could do or say anything else, Dr. Bender grabbed the golf bag from Julio while the strap was still across his shoulder. Julio knew too well what the doctor was about to do.

"No, Doc! No, Doc!" he pleaded but to no avail. Dr. Bender flung the bag toward the water, not realizing that Julio was still hanging on to it in a desperate attempt to keep the doctor from throwing it in the creek. Both Julio and the bag hit the water with a big splash. Dr. Bender quickly realized what he had done.

"Oh my God! I'm sorry, Julio!" he exclaimed as he then jumped into the creek to pull Julio out. Julio had sunk under the weight of the bag and could be seen struggling to swim under the crystal-clear waters of the creek.

Everyone else ran toward the two as they saw Dr. Bender swim toward Julio. He grabbed Julio, who was still hanging on to the bag and was coughing from the water he had inhaled. Dr. Bender held Julio as he pulled him out of the water. The others helped them both get back to solid ground as they heard Dr. Bender repeatedly say, "I'm sorry, Julio!"

After getting over the initial shock of the scene, Mr. Johnson began laughing out loud. Everyone else hesitated to laugh for fear that they would embarrass Dr. Bender and Julio, but when Dr. Bender too began laughing, they all joined in the fun, including Julio, who was lying on the ground soaking wet. After a moment of self-deprecation, Dr. Bender helped Julio up from the ground and told the others that he would take Julio back to the clubhouse to get dried up and asked them to continue the game without him.

Felipe had seen only two holes in his short caddying experience, but he had already seen more strange events than in his entire young life. He stood next to the creek frozen with amazement until Manuel nudged him to continue with the rest of the group. He followed without saying anything but kept thinking to himself, "Wow! I can't believe what I just saw!"

The rest of the round did not have the excitement of the first two holes, that is, until the group got to the fifteenth hole, which is the sixth hole the second time around. The hole is a short and straight par four but has creeks along both edges running all the way to the green. Joe was caddying for a player named Craig Seifert that day. Mr. Seifert tended to hook the ball, and today was no exception. When he hit his tee shot, the ball started on a path toward the middle of the fairway, but it quickly started turning left toward a group of trees next to the creek. They all heard the ball hit one of the trees, so they assumed that it did not go into the water. Once everyone in the group had hit their tee shots, Joe headed to the left side in the direction he thought he would find the ball. Mr. Seifert was not far behind.

When the two arrived in the general area where they had heard the ball strike a tree, they began looking. Mr. Seifert was rather nearsighted but refused to wear his glasses when he played golf. The glasses wouldn't stay on during the swing, he would say, so rather than have an optometrist adjust the glasses, he opted to play without them. He claimed he could still see the ball because the whiteness of it stood out against the grass and bare ground. After a few minutes of looking, he called out to Joe to say he had found the ball next to the tree that it had apparently hit and needed a six-iron to punch it out into the fairway. Joe obliged him but otherwise did not pay close attention to where the ball was lying.

Mr. Seifert stood for an inordinate amount of time by his ball while looking at it and then peering out through the trees in the direction of the fairway. What he didn't realize was that he had been standing on a red ant mound, and a great number of the creatures had already begun crawling up his legs, both inside and outside his pants. When he began feeling the stings of several of the ants, he looked more closely and saw what he thought were millions of them getting closer to his abdomen. He let out a frightful scream and started jumping up and down.

"Help me, Joe! Help me, Joe!" he kept shouting as he jumped, still trying to figure out what to do. Before Joe could get to him, Mr. Seifert started running toward the creek, and without hesitation, jumped in the water in an attempt to drown the attackers.

Joe dropped the bag he was holding and ran toward the edge of the creek while hearing Mr. Seifert call out for his help. Fortunately, where Mr. Seifert jumped, the water was only five feet deep, but at five feet nine inches tall, he was struggling to keep his head above the water line.

"Get a club and pull me up, Joe!" he pleaded to his caddie, and Joe immediately complied.

By now the other players had run over to the area of the ant attack along with the caddies. The boys were too shocked to say or do anything, but the players began to laugh loudly.

"What the hell was that, Craig?" Mr. Johnson asked through his laughter, but he got no response, as Joe was still trying to help Mr. Seifert out of the water.

When Mr. Seifert returned to the dry bank, he explained to the others why he had jumped in, and the laughter erupted again, as the players had only seen him jump but had not witnessed the attack. When the laughter died down, the men resumed their play. Mr. Seifert insisted on playing in wet clothes, much to the snickers of the boys.

The rest of the round proved boring compared to the earlier adventures, but Felipe nevertheless enjoyed himself. When it was over, and Manuel and Felipe were cleaning his clubs, Mr. Johnson approached them. He took out a dollar and two quarters and gave it to Manuel. Manuel immediately started to give Felipe the quarters, but Mr. Johnson stopped him. He then took out two more quarters from his pocket and gave them to Felipe as he watched Felipe give him a big smile with eyes wide open.

"Thank you, sir!" Felipe said to him as he walked away with his golf bag.

"Thank you, Mr. Johnson," Manuel repeated as Mr. Johnson walked away, waving his hand.

"So, whada ya think?" Manuel asked Felipe. "You think you ᴄan do this?"

"Yeah!" he quickly replied. "When can we do it again?"

"We'll come back tomorrow and see if you can pick up a bag by yourself!"

"All right!" Felipe exclaimed.

"But first, you're gonna have to learn to read the greens," Manuel professed. "Right now there's nobody on the number one green, so let's go over there."

"Okay!" Felipe replied.

They ran over to the first green, and Manuel began his lesson. He made Felipe look at the green from every side, showing how it was not flat but had different elevations and contours. Manuel took a golf ball and rolled it to show how the difference in the elevations made the ball go in different directions. He had Felipe feel the grass to help explain how the grass was growing and how the grain affected the putts. Felipe now began to understand how the ball could move left or right depending on which part of the green it started on and the location of the hole. It didn't take him long before he could tell Manuel which way the ball would roll when Manuel tested him by starting a ball in the direction of the hole from different spots on the green.

On the way home, Manuel explained to Felipe how the ball would fly differently when struck, depending on which club was used. He explained each club hit the ball a different distance—for instance, the long irons, the three through the six, made it go longer. Then there were the mid irons, which were used for shorter distances. For even shorter distances, there were the short irons and wedges. He gave Felipe the typical distances the ball would travel when hit by each club, beginning with the driver and ending with the wedge. Felipe just soaked in all of this knowledge but asked questions to learn more as his desire to return to the golf course kept growing more intense.

Manuel also explained to him that the object of the game was to get the ball in the hole with the fewest shots, or hits with the clubs. He answered Felipe's questions, such as, "What's a birdie and a bogey?" "What's a par and an eagle?" "What does it mean to be under par or over par?"

The hours before the next chance to caddy on the following day seemed too long for him. Yes, he wanted to be a caddie, but that was to make some money. That night all he could think about was that he wanted to learn how to hit the ball and play golf. That would be fun for him, he thought.

CHAPTER TWO

OVER THE COURSE OF the next several months, Felipe secured enough confidence in his abilities as a caddie that he was now being sought out by the players just like the other kids. He had memorized the swings of the players he regularly caddied for, such that he could determine the right club for them without being asked. He had also memorized what he felt his swing would look like if he decided to actually take a whack at the ball. He had gone through in his mind every night how he would swing the clubs, and each time he would send the golf ball flying on the perfect line toward the target. He could do it so well each time that he would beat the players he was caddying for, at least in his mind.

By the time Manuel and Felipe arrived at the course one particular day in August, several of the caddies had gathered by the practice range. Joe Trevino, the tallest and oldest of the kids, was showing the others his much-envied golf swing. His smooth, yet powerful swing was sending the golf ball in any direction he called out beforehand. The others were just watching in amazement. After hitting a handful of shots, Joe turned and handed the club, the only one owned among them all, to Mario Lomas.

Mario was the same age and height as Felipe, but his body was filled out more. He had black hair, which was slicked back in the style popular in those days, and darker skin. He knew the course very well, as he spent many hours there while his grandfather, who worked as a greens keeper, toiled to keep it in perfect condition for the members. This had allowed Mario to learn and practice the golf swing, but only while he was outside the view of the members.

Mario then showed his abilities with the golf ball with almost equal impressiveness. Felipe was definitely impressed, but while he had never actually swung a club before, in his own mind he was confident that he could make the swing and hit the ball. He thought that as soon as he could get the chance, he would try to take an assault on the ball. Before that could happen, one of the youngest of the group yelled out that he was next.

The kid was Higinio Vasquez, but since no one could pronounce his name, everybody called him Gene. Gene took the club from Mario and set himself up for his attempted swing. As Felipe saw his setup, something did not look right. The club that had been passed around among the boys was one made for right-handed players, but Gene was left-handed. He stood before the ball but with the club turned around so that the back side of the face of the club was facing the ball. How could he hit the ball? Felipe wondered. Gene made his swing from the left side and took a swipe at the ball. Though he made contact, the ball flew only three feet off the ground for about 20 yards but then rolled for another 100 yards. While Felipe was amazed and wondered why Gene swung that way, the other boys laughed and commented audibly. Gene, an eleven-year-old skinny but spunky kid, took the laughter in stride and kept on swinging.

"What is that?" one asked facetiously, referring to the left-sided swing.

"That's no way to swing a club!" shouted another. "You're left-handed?" Felipe asked Gene.

"Yeah," Gene answered as he turned to Felipe. "You can't swing right-handed?" Felipe followed up.

"No," Gene answered with a bit of embarrassment showing on his face. "I gotta swing this way 'cause we don't have a club for a leftie."

It was still somewhat confusing for Felipe, as he did not quite understand how it made a difference if you were left-handed or right-handed as far as the way the club was made. It was obvious that it did, but he said nothing more. Now it was his turn. He nervously took the club from Gene and gripped it just like he had seen Joe and Mario do it. He looked at the other boys and then stood next to the ball. He began his motion with the club in his hands and took a healthy swipe at the ball. Though it did not fly as well as those hit by Mario and Joe, it got airborne and traveled for a good distance. He pulled another ball from the pile of practice balls and got ready to hit it, but by then one of the other boys was yelling that some golfers were arriving, so they all scattered in the direction of the players, who would surely need a caddy. Felipe would have to wait for another chance to show the swing that he had developed in his mind every night before going to sleep.

This routine was repeated over and over for the next year. With each day, the boys got more and more familiar with the idiosyncrasies of each of the golfers who used their services. By now, each golfer had his preference of caddy and had no hesitation in rejecting the boisterous offers from the eager would-be servants and briskly calling out the name of the boy he wanted. One by one they were called out.

"Joe!" one yelled.

"Manuel!" another cried out. "Mario!" shouted another.

"Felipe!" followed yet another until all of the usual caddies picked up an assignment, including Gene, Lupe Felan, and several others.

When all of the golfers had selected their caddies and made arrangements for each foursome, they headed to the first tee. The caddies could hear the golfers making their bets for the day. That's what they did, as everyone knew that golf simply was no fun if you didn't have some money at stake. Some of the caddies would bet among themselves that their players would beat the others. It was like betting on which horse would win the race.

For the foursome consisting of Judge Lindsay, Horace Winn, O. B. Poole, and Phil Ricks, Manuel, Gene, Joe, and Mario would caddy.

Judge Lindsay was the county judge and had held office for years. He was an avid golfer, but what he boasted in enthusiasm, he lacked in talent. Despite his lack of abilities, he preferred to play with the better players. O. B. Poole was a local teacher, who enjoyed a single digit handicap. Mr. Winn was a civil service worker at the air force base situated just outside of town, while Mr. Ricks owned a furniture store and was involved in the local political scene.

As was usually the case, Mr. Poole had Mario on his bag. While Mario was wiping down the clubs, Mr. Poole came over to talk to him.

"Have you been working on your swing, Mario?" he asked.

"I've tried, sir, but it's hard 'cause we only have one club!" Mario replied.

Mr. Poole smiled, as he knew that what he was about to do was going to please himself almost as much as Mario. "You see that seven-iron in the bag that's different from the others?"

Mario looked through the bag and saw the club he was referring to. "This one?" he asked as he pulled a club out of the bag.

"Yeah! That's the one," Mr. Poole replied. "You can have it."

Mario was stunned and could not say anything. Finally he was able to ask, "It's mine?" with a look of amazement in his face.

"Yes, but you have to promise me that you will practice your swing with it. I want to see a good swing!"

"Thank you, sir!" Mario uttered excitedly as he carefully inspected the seven-iron. It was old, and rust had developed on parts of the metal head and shaft, and the grips were a bit worn. That didn't matter, as it looked like a brand-new one to Mario.

"Keep it in the bag, and you can take it after the round," Mr. Poole instructed.

"Yessir!" Mario responded as he placed the club back into the bag and began walking toward the first tee box with the bag strap on his shoulder. He stopped when he realized that saying it once was not enough. "Thank you, Mr. Poole! Thank you very much!" he repeated with a big smile.

"You're welcome, Mario! Now, let's go take their money!" he said with a smile, nodding his head in the direction of the other members of the foursome.

"Yessir!" Mario exclaimed while continuing on to the first tee box.

The foursome teed off and began their play for the day without much excitement or anything out of the ordinary occurring. That is, until the fifth hole. Judge Lindsay was a very anxious fellow, and sometimes he had a tendency not to wait for the others to hit their shots before he began his walk to where he thought his ball had landed. A creek dissected the fifth hole, which had a dogleg to the right, just about ninety degrees. This forced players to hit a mid to long iron off the tee and then hit their second shot over the creek to an elevated green about the same distance as their first.

Judge Lindsay had hit his tee shot toward the left side of the fairway, which didn't present much of a problem, although it left him with a long shot to the green. The others were just about in the middle of the fairway, with a clear view of the green. But before they arrived at their balls, Judge Lindsay took a big swipe at his ball with a four-wood. As was usually the case, he sent a screaming ball left over the creek but toward some trees that lined the fairway approaching the green. He mumbled something incomprehensible, expressing his disgust with the result, and walked briskly down the path toward the trees before any of the other players could hit their shots.

Gene, who was caddying for him that day, quickly followed the judge, even though he knew that the other golfers had not yet hit their shots. Two of the golfers in the fairway hit their shots on the green, but before the fourth one could swing away, Mario noticed Judge Lindsay rustling about in the trees in search of his ball. He quickly informed Mr. Poole, who then yelled to the judge to be aware that Horace was about to hit the ball. Mr. Winn also yelled to him to get behind a tree and wait until the ball was struck. As Mr. Winn addressed his ball, he shook his head in amazement, nodding his disapproval of the judge's impatience. He apparently failed to contain his own emotions, as he struck the ball poorly, sending it on an unintended path directly toward the area where the judge was hiding. Everyone yelled "fore" immediately, but rather than remain in his safe haven, Judge Lindsay peered out right at the moment that the ball arrived on his mouth with the violence and force that golf balls tend to carry when violently struck. Everyone could hear the sound of the "whack" as the ball struck his teeth and cheekbones, followed by the frightening yell of the judge as the pain struck and blood began spewing out of his mouth. They all rushed over to him, and when they arrived, Judge Lindsay was on his knees, holding his mouth in a weak attempt to stop the bleeding. Mr. Ricks pulled out a handkerchief from his pants pocket and told the judge to lie on his back on the ground as he pressed the cloth against his mouth. The ball had split the top lip, leading the players to urge the judge to get to a doctor immediately, as he apparently would need some stitches to close the wound and keep the blood loss at a minimum.

"I'm all right! I'm all right!" the judge kept saying as he tried to get up. The blood kept leaking out of his mouth and onto his clothes. It appeared quite worse than it actually was but was nonetheless frightening.

"You need to get to a doctor, judge!" Mr. Ricks stated insistently. "Hell, I'll take you!" he said emphatically as he grabbed the judge by the arm to help him to the parking lot. He ordered Gene to grab his bag and follow them along as he walked with the judge, who was still claiming he was all right and could continue playing.

The other two players stood silently at the area where the errant golf ball had attempted to occupy the same space as the judge's mouth, and although neither said a word, they could tell they were both pondering the same question, "Do we continue playing?"

The caddies stood silently as well by their players' side with the strongest urge to laugh. While they felt bad for the judge, they considered the incident quite funny, but out of respect for him, they resisted the temptation to display their true reaction. Suddenly, the two players looked at each other and began laughing hysterically, such that the caddies couldn't help but join in.

"What are the odds," Mr. Winn began to ask laughingly and continued, "that I would hit the ball and hit the judge right on the kisser?"

The question didn't need an answer beyond the laughter that could be heard coming from the trees near the green of the fifth hole.

CHAPTER THREE

AFTER COMPLETING A ROUND of caddying one day, several of the caddies gathered around the first tee box at the urging of one of the older boys. He had suggested that since no one was on the course and it was late in the afternoon, they should go out and play a round of golf themselves. They all understood that they couldn't play golf on the course they knew so well, and no one had tried before.

"I don't think we can do that!" warned Mario.

"Why not?" the boy asked defiantly.

"'Cause we're caddies!" replied Joe.

"Yeah, we'll get in trouble!" Felipe followed.

"Nah, we won't!" the boy insisted. "No one's gonna see us anyway!"

Joe, Mario, Felipe, Lupe, and Gene looked at each other with a fear in their eyes, but they couldn't come up with an explanation that would make sense to the boy. They just knew that they could not do what he suggested. Before any of them could say anything, one of the other caddies had placed a ball on a tee of the first tee box and was getting ready to swing. Just then a member who had just finished hitting balls on the practice range and was heading to his car saw the gathering and approached them.

"What's going on?" he inquired as they all looked at him but could say nothing.

"Uh, nothing, sir!" the defiant boy sheepishly replied.

The man looked at all of them one by one, seeing if anyone would volunteer the truth that he suspected he was not getting from the one who answered. The extended silence was broken when he asked," You boys weren't thinkin' about playing on our course, were you?"

No one said a word, but the boy who had placed a ball on a tee knocked it off with his foot in a vain attempt to hide his intentions.

"No, sir!" the boy replied.

"'Cause you know you boys aren't allowed to play!" the man stated sternly.

"Yessir! We know that, sir!" Joe interjected. "Only members can play, and we ain't members, sir! We know that!"

"Yessir! We know that!" Mario chimed in while the other boys nodded their heads in agreement.

"We let you boys caddy here, but that's all. If you think you want to play, you're gonna have to find someplace else for that! Playing's for members only! Now you best be getting off the course, since there's no more caddying for you to do today, all right?"

"Yessir!" they all said in unison and began walking away.

The man stood in his place until he saw that all of the boys had physically walked off the grounds of the country club.

Although disappointed, the caddies fully understood why it was that they could not play the course where they worked. Yes, they knew that they could not play because they were not members, but they also were well aware that they could never be members. Yet they all wanted to play the game. None of them had to say anything, for the strong desire suppressed by the circumstances was evident in their faces. They had figured out a basic swing, and though they had learned to strike the ball in the intended manner, they could not really say that they knew how to play, as there was no place where they could put their swings to the test and see if they could take it from tee to green and actually score.

"What are we going to do now?" asked Felipe as they walked across the part of San Felipe Creek that meandered through the public park near the course.

"I wish there was someplace we could play," lamented Gene.

"Yeah! We should have our own country club," suggested Joe.

"That's right, and only Mexicans can be members," added Lupe.

"I know what we can do!" shouted Mario. "We can make our own course!"

The others stared at him but couldn't come up with anything to say, at least not for a brief moment. They all wondered if it could be done, but no one had a doubt that it was a good idea to make their own place to play.

"How do we do that?" asked Joe.

"We could do it at *el llanito*. You know, the flat area of land on the other side of Margarita by Garza Street," Mario began to explain.

"But there's a lot of *mesquites* there," Lupe pointed out.

"We'll just have to cut some down to make a fairway," Mario replied. "But how?" asked Gene.

"*Con hachas!*" Joe said. "You have an *hacha* at home, don't you?" "Yeah. My dad has one," Gene offered.

"I can get one too," Mario stated.

"But what do we do about greens?" Felipe asked. "We have no grass to plant and no mowers to cut it with!"

Everyone looked puzzled, as they felt Felipe had a good point. But then Joe broke the silence.

"We don't need a green," he suggested. We just have to clear a round area and make it hard so the ball will roll. We'll make a hole in the middle, and we have our green!"

"You mean our brown," Gene corrected as they all laughed in agreement.

"All right then," Mario declared. "We will make our own course and call it *El Llanito* Country Club."

"Yeah and no *bolillos* allowed!" Lupe added.

"That's right!" they all affirmed while continuing to walk to their respective homes.

"Hey, let's do it tomorrow 'cause it's Monday and the club is closed," Mario insisted.

"Yeah! Let's do it!" Joe agreed. "Everybody bring an *hacha!*" he ordered.

"Okay!" they all replied.

The next day they carried out their plans. With axes in hand, they determined which mesquite trees and bushes to knock down to clear an area that would be used as a fairway. Based on their knowledge of the holes at San Felipe Country Club, where they worked, they designed a hole about 300 yards in length. When they had cleared enough trees and bushes to create the semblance of a fairway, they moved on to the area where they would "build" their "green."

With some hoes and axes, they cleared a circular area about twenty feet in diameter to serve as the green, even though it was completely brown. They scraped the topsoil from this area to expose the surface made harder by the prominent caliche. When they were all convinced that the ground was clear and hard enough, they cut a hole in the middle, and to make the hole round, they buried a small coffee can close to the usual specifications of a real golf hole. Joe then took his pocketknife and cut one of the limbs of a mesquite tree that they had cut down and sliced off the protruding small limbs. Once he was convinced that he had a clean and straight stick, he took an old handkerchief from his pocket and tied it to the stick. He then placed the stick with the "flag" in the hole, but it would not stay up. He pondered for a moment, and then an idea popped into his head. With his pocketknife he punched a hole in the bottom center of the can just big enough to accommodate the end of the mesquite stick. He again placed the flag into the hole, and this time it stood straight up, thereby marking the hole on the "green." With this act, the boys proclaimed the creation of El Llanito Country Club, and the five were accepted as the first, and only, members.

Every day after they had finished caddying for the golfers at the club, they rushed over to their "course" and played their game. They would take turns with the two or three clubs they owned between them to attempt to hole their balls on their green. In the afternoons once school started in the fall and every day that they had no caddying jobs at the club, they continued their play on their own country club.

But hitting balls from the grassless ground was different from hitting them from the nice grass of an actual course. It presented a unique challenge for them all. Not having grass required them to pick the ball cleanly off the ground so that the club would not slam down against the hard surface and bounce up. They all knew that if they didn't do this, their hands would hurt when the club hit the hard ground. The sting of a mishit was not pleasant and would linger for a while. Not to mention that the ball would not get airborne, as the bounce would cause the bottom edge of the club to catch the upper half of the ball, thus producing a "topper."

Since the club had only one hole, they would play it eighteen times, each time from a different starting point, so as to make it a different hole. Putting was also a challenge. Although they had made every effort to smooth out the green, the surface was not flat or smooth at all. The ball would roll left and right, up and down, as it followed each bump or depression present. But having only one hole did have its advantages. After playing it so many times, they each knew exactly what the ball was going to do as it rolled toward the "cup" from every conceivable angle.

After several months, they decided to lengthen the hole by clearing a few more trees and bushes. They even "built" a slight bend to the hole to make it a par five and increase the challenge. El Llanito Country Club now had one master hole that could serve as a par three, a par four, and a par five, depending on where you teed up the ball each time. It was a par-seventy-two layout that very few people knew about but that served as a sanctuary for five young golfers who had developed a keen interest in and love for the game. They were not going to be kept from playing just because they were not members of the "real" club.

CHAPTER FOUR

Until Joe Mitchell became the golf pro at the San Felipe Country Club, the caddies never even thought about playing anywhere else but at El Llanito, and they were content with that. Mario was the only one who could sneak in some play on the real course, in the early morning hours when he followed his grandfather as he did his job. Just before his grandfather began to cut the grass on the tee box, Mario would tee up a golf ball and hit it toward the green. He would then run to the green, or the ball if it hadn't reached the green, and hit it again before his grandfather got to the green on his tractor to mow it. He did the same thing on the next eight holes while his grandfather mowed each of them. He could only play nine holes, as this was when he had the cover of the early dawn to protect his secret play, but it was enough to satisfy his cravings for the game. He never feared getting caught, as no one ever saw him doing it, or so he thought.

One day after finishing the ninth hole, he waited for his grandfather to finish mowing the green. Then he jumped on the tractor with his grandfather and headed toward the equipment shed. As he was helping his grandfather clean up the mower by the shed, a man on a golf cart approached them. He stopped the cart near the tractor and got off the cart.

"You must be 'Graygoreeo,'" he said to Mario's grandfather.

"Yessir!" was the reply. "I'm Gregorio Reyes."

"I'm the new golf pro at the club, and I was going around the course checking out the conditions. Looks good, Graygoreeo. Thanks."

"Thank you, sir!" the grandfather replied.

"I'll be talking to you later. Keep up the good work," he said as he climbed back into the cart. "Nice swing, young man!" he said to a shocked Mario.

"Thank you, sir," Mario muttered, realizing that he had been discovered. "Thank you!" he tried again but with more volume.

"See you around!" the man added as he drove away.

"Am I in trouble, Grandpa?" Mario asked with his voice shaking. He knew that not only would they get after him, but maybe he had also gotten his grandfather in hot water.

"Don't worry about it, *mijo*. Nothing's gonna happen," his grandfather reassured him. "You better get ready for work. Golfers will be getting here soon."

"Yes. I guess I better go," Mario acknowledged and began running toward the parking lot.

By the time he got there, all of the other caddies were already waiting for the golfers who would be hiring them for the round that day. For some unexplainable reason, the players for whom the boys regularly looped did not play, so someone else would have to pick them today. Joe was selected by Bennett Harlow, whom everyone knew was a notorious cheapskate. Mario was picked by a newcomer, and no one knew much about him. He brought his son, who was not much older than Gene, the caddie chosen to carry his bag. Felipe was the most unfortunate one; he ended up having to caddie for one of the grouchiest members, Landon Pierce.

Felipe took a big breath and quietly picked up the man's golf bag as the others looked at him with a sympathetic gaze. While he knew that Mr. Pierce was not his favorite player to work for, Felipe was determined to do a good job and try to earn a good tip. He also knew that this would be difficult.

The round began with little, if any, significant problems, until the fourth hole. Felipe and his boss for the day were assessing the next shot to the green. About five paces short of the green was a creek that ran across the fairway, so they both knew that the shot had to be long enough to clear the fast-running water that was notorious for sucking in golf balls. Felipe had calculated that his boss had 133 yards to the front edge of the green and 142 to the center, where the flag was situated. He relayed this information to Mr. Pierce and repeated it again when Mr. Pierce asked Felipe if he was sure.

"I suggest an eight-iron, sir," Felipe said as he handed him the eight-iron.

"What, you don't think I can get a nine there?" Mr. Pierce asked.

"I think it's an eight, sir," Felipe repeated in a soft and respectful tone.

The man pondered for a minute and then barked his order, "Give me a nine!"

Although Felipe normally avoided being hired by Mr. Pierce, he was quite familiar with his swing and the yardages he usually hit with his clubs. He again tried to convince him to change his mind. "I really think you should hit an eight, sir," he pleaded.

"Just give me the goddamn nine, boy!"

Felipe quickly pulled the nine-iron from the bag and handed it to the man as the other caddies looked at him, trying to give him a sign to confirm that he was right. Felipe returned the eight-iron to the bag and moved away from Mr. Pierce, who was practicing his swing. With no one making a sound, the man stood by the ball and prepared his swing. It appeared that the man had his doubts about the club selection as he swung harder than normal. The mighty swing he took moved the clubhead against the ball, but the sound it made indicated to Felipe and the others that he had slightly missed it, hitting the ground about a quarter of an inch behind the ball.

"He hit it fat!" Felipe thought in his mind. He was right. Although the ball had a good flight toward the flag, it did not have the distance to get there. As gravity returned the golf ball toward the earth, it suddenly disappeared between the front and back banks of the creek.

"Shit!" the man uttered in disgust, throwing down the club to add emphasis to his anger. He turned to Felipe and expressed the ruling he had foolishly made in his mind, "You're such a dumb fuck! You gave me the wrong yardage!"

Felipe was stunned, but he did not hesitate to disagree with him. "No, sir. My yardage was right!" he exclaimed. "And I'm not a dumb fuck!"

Felipe grabbed the golf bag and ran toward the club that had been victimized by its vituperative owner. Joe walked over to Felipe and tried to assure him that he was not wrong about his yardage and that the man had simply hit it fat and should have hit the eight-iron as Felipe had suggested. He had to speak quietly so as not to be heard by the man and the other players and have them think that he and Felipe were being disrespectful. Felipe arrived at the edge of the creek and took out a golf ball from the bag, as the man would have to take a drop in order to continue playing the hole. He then pulled out the pitching wedge and handed it to the player. This time the man did not question the choice of clubs, but everyone could tell that he was still steaming over the previous shot.

The man failed to take his time and a practice swing. He swung and this time he "skulled" the shot, causing the ball to run through the green, almost hitting Joe's boss, who was on the other side assessing his putt. The player quickly jumped out of the way as Mr. Pierce hollered, "Sorry, Ben!"

After Bennett succeeded in dodging the ball, he shouted, "Jeez, Landon! Take it easy!"

Mr. Pierce mumbled something unintelligible and walked around to find the footbridge allowing him to cross over the creek and get to the green. He remained speechless, as he was still not over the frustration of having hit a very poor shot. Felipe walked briskly right behind him with the bag in tow.

The ball had run past about 30 yards behind the green. This meant that the frustrated golfer would have to hit a high shot to reach and stay on the green. Instead of doing this, he again skulled the ball, causing it to roll very quickly up onto the green and continue across the front side and into the creek again. The club that hit the ball into the water quickly followed it into the creek amid expletives uttered by the now-boiling, red-faced golfer.

"I'm done on this hole!" Mr. Pierce yelled to the group. "Just give me an X on the card!"

By this time, Felipe couldn't decide if he was glad to see his boss encounter such misfortune or afraid that he would continue to suffer the misdirected verbal jabs from him. He assumed that the abuse would go on if he didn't make some effort to retrieve the drowning wedge from the creek. He carefully lowered himself to an area on the same level of the creek that was dry. Before he could reach for the club, he heard from his golfer.

"Leave the fucking thing in there, boy!"

Felipe ignored him and grabbed the club, which fortunately was only halfway submerged in the creek. "I got it!" Felipe replied, holding the wedge up so that the boss could see it. The owner said nothing, but Felipe placed it back in the bag after wiping it dry.

The rest of the day didn't get any better, but at least it did not get worse. Not for Felipe anyway. For sixteen holes Joe's golfer hardly said a word. Joe had handed him a club on each shot without any comment from Mr. Harlow. Joe assumed that he had so far been able to satisfy his boss on this day, and he might get a decent tip at the end of the round.

On the seventeenth hole, the par five that Mr. Harlow never had been able to reach in two, Joe handed him a five-iron to follow the 235-yard drive he had hit from the tee. Joe figured that his boss would want to lay up to about 100 yards short of the hole, as he usually did. This time, though, he wanted a three-wood from Joe, even though he was about 255 yards to the middle of the green and he couldn't hit that distance with his driver. But Joe had seen what Felipe had endured when he disagreed earlier in the round with his golfer.

"Yessir!" Joe responded to the request as he handed him the three-wood. He looked at Felipe, who was shaking his head in disbelief, and then Joe nodded in agreement. He knew exactly what Felipe was thinking. They waited for the inevitable unpleasant result.

With a mighty whack at the ball, Mr. Harlow sent the ball on a slicing path toward the tee box of the sixteenth hole and the creek just to the right of it. Another ball found the minnows' home in San Felipe Creek.

"Crap!" was the only thing Mr. Harlow had to say as he threw the club down near where Joe was standing and walked away.

Joe said nothing but grabbed the club, placed it in the bag, and started walking behind his boss. There was no denying that the ball had bounced into the creek. By the time Joe arrived at the area where he figured the ball had made its entry into the water, Mr. Harlow was standing with his hand out. Joe had already pulled another ball from the bag, so he handed it to him without either saying a word. The golfer then dropped it behind his right shoulder and was ready to hit his next shot. Joe handed him the pitching wedge without being asked, and Mr. Harlow took it without questioning the choice of clubs. Unlike Mr. Pierce, Mr. Harlow managed to regain his composure enough to hit a decent shot onto the green and then dropped the club next to Joe's feet.

Joe said nothing, but he began to suspect his player was not very pleased with him, even though he'd done nothing wrong.

The players finished getting their balls into the hole without further incident and moved on to the final hole, a par three that would also require hitting a shot that would have to clear the creek again. For the 150 yards that the ball would have to fly, Joe pulled out a six-iron for Mr. Harlow to hit.

"You don't think I can get there with a seven?" he asked Joe.

"I think it's a six 'cause we got a little wind in our face, sir," Joe replied.

Mr. Harlow looked at it but decided to ignore the flapping of the flag on the pole marking the eighteenth hole. "I'll hit a seven!" he said as he grabbed it from the bag and moved to the tee box to begin his pre-shot routine.

When he was ready to hit, Joe turned to Felipe and the other caddies, who seemed puzzled by what was going on. They all knew Mr. Harlow couldn't get a seven home and never had tried before when they caddied for someone in his group. Even though the strike of the ball sounded solid, the ball sailed toward the green but fell short, just as they all expected. The golfer dropped the club by Joe's feet and tugged abruptly at his glove to remove it in disgust but said nothing. Joe quietly picked up the club and returned it to its place in the bag. Something was amiss, he thought. He had an idea what was about to happen.

Once the other players had all hit their tee shots, they walked across the bridge and headed uphill toward the green, with the caddies right behind them. Nobody said anything. When the players had all holed out, the caddies made sure that the equipment was properly cleaned and returned to its rightful place as they always did and then waited for their players to retrieve their bags. This is when they would get paid.

Mr. Harlow approached Joe, who was standing by his bag, and handed him what was supposed to be his well-earned tip. "I don't think you were much help to me today, boy!" he said to Joe as he handed him a single coin.

Joe looked at it and realized that it was a dime, a much lower payment than what he was accustomed to getting. Joe got incensed but tried very hard not to show his anger or disrespect. He knew that if any caddie was seen as being disrespectful to his golfer, word would spread quickly, and jobs would be limited, if there were any at all.

"Sir," Joe began. "If you don't want to pay me, that's fine. But don't tell me I did a poor job 'cause I know I did a good job for you!" he proclaimed as he tried to hand the dime back to the man.

The man said nothing but did not take the dime back. He just walked away, knowing that he had just been unfair to a kid, despite not admitting it verbally. The absence of any words confirmed in Joe's mind that he was right and that the boss just wanted to stiff him out of his pay. He tried as best he could to forbid the tears that wanted to come out from doing so, not because he had only received a measly dime, but because of the idea that somebody would think that he had not been a good caddy that day when he knew otherwise.

"What did he give you?" asked Gene who was holding three quarters in his opened hand.

"A damn dime!" Joe answered as he threw it in the direction of the creek. "I don't need his stinking money!"

"Well, I got a quarter from old man Pierce," Felipe offered with disappointment in his voice. "But I think I'll keep it. Come on!" he said to Joe while patting him on the arm. "I'll buy you a soda on the way home."

"You? Buy him a soda?" Gene asked facetiously. "That's a miracle!"

"Hey!" Felipe shouted as he slapped Gene on the arm.

"Let's go play at our club!" Joe suggested, having gotten over the insult that had been heaved upon him by an ungrateful boss.

"Yeah!" they all hailed in agreement.

They all took off running with the few clubs they owned between them and headed to El Llanito Country Club, stopping only long enough for a soda at *El Farolito* store. It had been a terrible day for the caddies at the course, but it would now be a good afternoon for the young golfers of El Llanito.

CHAPTER FIVE

Aᴿᴛᴇʀ ᴄᴏᴍᴘʟᴇᴛɪɴɢ ᴀ ʀᴏᴜɴᴅ of caddying one Saturday afternoon in 1954, it was time to go "shopping" again for some golf balls.

"Let's go get some golf balls, guys!" Joe yelled out to the others as he made a dash toward the creek on the first hole right by the fence.

Earlier in the day and before the round had begun, Joe, Mario, and Gene had hidden their homemade ball retrievers under some leaves by the fence. They were the tools that would secure for them "new" golf balls to both sell and keep for their use. The retrievers were long bamboo poles neatly trimmed of all leaves, roughly eight feet long. The circular ends of the poles had been hollowed out, and slits had been cut across from ten through two o'clock with another slit from eight through four o'clock, if you looked straight at the opening. Then one piece of bamboo about six inches long and a quarter inch wide was slid into the cut at ten o'clock, extending through the cut at two o'clock, with a similar-sized stick placed in the cut at eight o'clock and extending through the cut at four o'clock.

A piece of thin rope or leather was then tied around the pole about six inches away from the end to secure the two thin sticks to the pole. This opened the end of the pole enough to allow a golf ball to slide into the opening but also forced the flexible ends to grip the ball and keep it secure until it was manually released. When Joe and the others spotted a ball in the water, they would extend the pole, modified end first, into the water and force the end against the ball. The force applied against the ball sitting in the creek bottom forced it into the opening, and it stayed there until they removed the pole from the water and took the ball out. A simple but quite effective contraption.

Mario and Joe had taken their retrievers and decided to search for balls in the part of the creek that ran along the right side of the second fairway. As they began their "shopping," Joe noticed a group had approached the first green, which was a short distance from the second tee box.

"Hey, Mario!" Joe called out. "I bet Mr. Gurvis hits his ball into the creek!" Joe said as he pointed to the group on the first green. Mario just laughed, nodding in agreement. "Let's move over behind that tree," Joe suggested. Both of them moved and hid behind a tree on the edge of the creek and waited for the group to tee off.

When the players moved to the second tee box, the boys saw and heard the first and second balls hit the fairway in the typical landing area. Then it was Mr. Gurvis's turn. As Joe predicted, the ball landed a few feet from where they were hiding and took one jump right into the creek. Joe smiled at Mario and then quickly walked over to the edge where the ball went in. He lowered his pole once he spotted the ball and speared the ball.

"Gotcha!" was Joe's only expression. By the time Mr. Gurvis made his way toward them, Joe had the ball in his extended hand. "Here's your ball, Mr. Gurvis!"

As he pulled a coin from his pocket, Mr. Gurvis said, "Thank you, son!" He handed Joe a dime as Joe placed the ball in its owner's hand.

Joe and Mario waited until Mr. Gurvis and the other players hit their shots toward the second green. Unfortunately for Mr. Gurvis, another creek bounded the left edge of the second fairway, forcing the second shot to the green to fly over it. Joe was betting that Mr. Gurvis couldn't get it across. Again Mr. Gurvis took a swing that sent the ball into this second creek. Joe paid close attention to the flight of the ball and saw where it got wet once more. He ran toward the second creek with his pole and before too long, he had again liberated the poorly hit ball from the creek.

When Mr. Gurvis's group finished with the second hole, Joe and Mario were waiting by the green. Upon seeing the boys, Mr. Gurvis pulled another dime from his pocket and gave it to Joe in exchange for his ball. No words needed to be spoken.

Joe looked at Mario, and they both smiled. "Let's go to the number four green," he directed Mario. "I betcha he hits it in the creek in front of the green."

The number three hole had no water in play, so Joe's suggestion was right on. They had to wait patiently as the group negotiated its way through the green on number two and then hole number three. Mario looked all along the creek fronting the fourth hole and found a couple of balls sent in there earlier in the day.

Finally, the group with Mr. Gurvis approached the area where they had hit their tee shots on the fourth hole. Now they had to hit their second shots, so they had to go over the water in order to get to the green. Joe and Mario were hiding behind a tall pecan tree by the fourth green, waiting. They saw Mr. Gurvis hit the shot, which started on a good line.

"It's got a chance to get over," Mario whispered. "Nahh," Joe challenged.

Sure enough, the ball came up short, hit the edge of the bank closest to the green, and bounced back into the water.

"Damn!" everyone heard Mr. Gurvis yell.

Joe then made his way to the area where he had seen the ball go in, and again he speared the ball with his bamboo pole. When he pulled it out of the water, the golf ball was clearly attached to the end. He then waited for Mr. Gurvis to cross the bridge and walk to where he was waiting. When Mr. Gurvis got close, he stopped and looked at Joe. He remained silent for a moment before reaching again into his pocket.

"You know what, son?" he asked rhetorically as Joe handed him the ball.

"You keep it! I already paid you more than what the damn thing is worth!" He handed Joe another dime and walked away without the ball.

Joe and Mario looked at each other, smiled, and then ran toward the creek along the fifth hole. They weren't expecting any more money from Mr. Gurvis but decided to wait there until the group got by. Even if none of them hit it in the water, they were sure to find other victims of bad swings.

"Is it a good one?" Mario asked Joe, pointing at the ball previously owned by Mr. Gurvis.

"Nah! It's one of those cheapies I've seen at the drug store!" "You gonna keep it?"

"Nah! I'll sell it for a dime and make forty cents off this sucker!" He threw the ball in his bag and positioned himself behind some trees while they waited for it to be clear. They had a little more shopping to do this afternoon in the creeks of San Felipe.

CHAPTER SIX

CRITICAL CHANGES IN SOCIETY come after someone takes a bold step toward challenging the status quo. Minor as these steps may seem initially, the effects are many times major, as they lead to the eventual unraveling of the attitudes of those resisting the changes to begin with. The attitudes toward Mexican Americans' role in the game of golf within the San Felipe Country Club and in the City of Del Rio began to change when on a day in 1955, Joe Mitchell, the golf pro at San Felipe, saw Mario again hitting balls off the number four tee box as Mr. Mitchell was driving his golf cart around the course in the early morning. He stopped short of the number three green behind some trees so as not to be noticed by Mario. He watched Mario take several swings and made special note of the balance and smoothness of Mario's hands and arms as they rotated around his small frame while the club solidly struck each ball. After striking a handful of balls, Mario took off running in the direction of the landing area. He set up again and began hitting them back toward where he had hit them first. When Mario ran toward their landing area again, Joe Mitchell revealed himself by driving his cart toward Mario.

"I've been looking for you, Muhreeo!" he shouted to him.

Mario was startled and immediately began to fear the worst. He could say nothing as the fear froze his tongue.

"Have you been playing the course, son?" he asked.

Mario shook his head from side to side in response but still could not muster any words.

"No?" Mr. Mitchell asked in disbelief.

Mario finally spoke up. "No, sir!" he stated firmly. "We are not allowed to play, sir!" he insisted.

"Well then how did you develop that swing of yours? You must be playing somewhere!" he said in a seemingly accusatorial tone.

"Ahh yessir, but not here!" Mario professed.

Mr. Mitchell was puzzled, as he knew there was no other place to play golf in town. After pondering Mario's claim, he asked, "Well then, where have you been playing, son?"

Mario thought for a moment, as he could not remember if he and his fellow members had vowed to keep their golf club a secret. He recalled that his father and grandfather had always stressed that he should be straight and truthful to his elders, and this made him feel compelled to reveal his membership in El Llanito.

"In El Llanito!" he blurted out.

"The what?" the puzzled pro asked.

Mario knew now that he had to give up the details of their golf secret in order to prove that he was not playing at the club. "We play at El Llanito Country Club, Mr. Mitchell, not here at the club."

A surprised but curious Mr. Mitchell just had to ask for those details. "Where is this El yaneedo Country Club?" he asked. "I've never heard of it!"

Mario began to explain. "It's a course we made near where we live ..."

"Who's we?" Mr. Mitchell interrupted.

"Me and the other caddies, sir," Mario replied.

"How did you make this course?" Mr. Mitchell asked.

"We cut down some trees and bushes to clear the ground and make a fairway," Mario continued.

"Did you plant grass on your fairway?"

"No, sir. We don't have money for grass," Mario confessed.

"What about a green? Did you make a green with grass?"

"No, sir. We didn't have money for grass for the green either."

"So what did you do for a green?" Mr. Mitchell continued asking.

"We just scraped the ground with hoes and made a circle on the ground. Then we made a little round hole and put a can in the hole for our cup."

Mr. Mitchell spent a moment thinking about what he had just

heard. While holding his hand to his chin and gazing upward, he tried to imagine this little course. "How long is your golf hole?" he asked.

"Oh, … it's about 430 *pazos*, but we play it three different ways …"

"Four hundred thirty what?"

"Oh, ahh, paces," Mario translated.

"Oh! So about 430 yards?" he asked.

"Yessir! More or less."

"I see."

"Like I said, we play it from three places."

"What do you mean?" Mr. Mitchell asked.

"We go to about 100 paces to play it as a par three. Then we go to about 350 paces to play it as a par four and then around 420 paces to play it as a par five," Mario explained.

"I see now!" Mr. Mitchell uttered, showing that he was impressed. "And who has the course record on your club?" he asked with a facetious smile.

"Joe can play nine holes in thirty-three, and I can do it in thirty-five!" Mario claimed proudly.

"Really?" Mr. Mitchell asked in amazement. "That's quite impressive!" He thought for while and then returned to the reason he was looking for Mario to begin with. "Do you and the other caddies want to play at the club?"

Mario was stunned by the question but could not figure out what Mr. Mitchell was getting at. "Yessir," he said hesitatingly. "But we don't want to get in trouble."

"Ohh! You're not going to get in any trouble. I've talked to some of the members about you and the other caddies. They all say good things about you boys," he reassured him. "Tell you what we're going to do. You boys can play on the course but only on Mondays when the club is closed, provided that you behave and take good care of the course."

"Wow!" was all that Mario could muster in his shock and excitement.

Mr. Mitchell smiled and winked an eye at Mario. "As soon as the other boys get here this morning, we'll have a meeting with the caddies, and I'll tell you my rules. Okay?"

"Yessir!" Mario replied excitedly and with a big grin on his face.

"All right then. I'll see you by the first tee in a bit," he said and then drove away on his cart.

"Did you hear that, Grandpa?" Mario asked, turning to his grandfather with eyes wide open.

"Yes, mijo. I heard. Just remember. You and the other caddies need to make sure that you do as Mr. Mitchell says, okay?"

"Yes, Grandpa. I will!"

Mario then ran toward the caddy gathering area, where several of the boys were already waiting to get a job for the day. As he approached them, his big grin signaled to the rest that he was excited about something, and it didn't take long for them to begin their inquiry.

"What's going on?" Joe asked.

"Yeah, why the big smile?" Gene followed.

Mario could not contain his excitement and felt compelled to reveal the news he had wanted to keep secret until Mr. Mitchell arrived.

"Mr. Mitchell is gonna let us play!" Mario shouted.

"What do you mean?" Felipe asked as they all got closer to hear what Mario was about to explain.

"Mr. Mitchell said the caddies can play the course, but only on Mondays. And we got to follow the rules," Mario stated excitedly and almost out of breath.

"You mean we get to play on a real golf course now?" Lupe wondered out loud.

"Yes!" Mario replied. "Mr. Mitchell is gonna come and tell us all about it."

"When? Gene asked.

"In a little while, he said," Mario answered.

"No," Gene responded. "When do we get to play?"

"Oh! I don't know. But Mr. Mitchell will be here to tell us."

"Wow! Does that mean no more Llanito?" Lupe asked.

"Of course not!" Joe quickly proclaimed. "We just get to play here on Mondays. The rest of the week we only have El Llanito to play on."

"Oh. Yeah," Lupe agreed.

While the boys muttered expressions of surprise to themselves, Mr. Mitchell showed up and was quickly noticed. Mario nudged Joe, who was standing next to him, and without saying anything, pointed to Mr. Mitchell. The others then gathered around Joe and Mario in anticipation of what they were about to hear.

"I see Muhreeo's told you boys," Mr. Mitchell began. "I got the club members to agree to allow you boys to play the course on Mondays when it is closed to all play. But!" he stressed. "You boys will have to follow my strict rules!" With that, he began explaining what he expected of each caddy being granted the privilege of playing at this exclusive club. The boys listened attentively as they looked at Mr. Mitchell with smiles that said they'd agree to anything to be allowed to play on a real golf course. They would have to fix any divots they made on the course and try to fix others they saw. They would also have to fix all the marks on the greens made by landing balls. Any trash seen on the course would have to be picked up and placed in the trash cans. These were some of his rules. When he finished explaining them, he asked, "Do you boys understand these rules?"

"Yessir," they all said in unison.

"Do you all promise to live up to these rules?" he continued. "Yessir," they repeated.

He tried to get eye contact with each of the boys to somehow assure himself that he had gotten through to all of the caddies. He was pleased with the reception to his announcement. He enjoyed a feeling of satisfaction, knowing that he had just followed his own sense of doing what was fair and right.

"Well then," he continued, "let's get ready for today. The golfers are waiting, so go out and do a good job today!"

The boys all headed for the first tee without any hesitation. Today nothing, not even the most demanding player, would damper their spirits.

CHAPTER SEVEN

DESPITE KNOWING THEY WOULD not receive a positive reception, two men showed up at the country club's office one day in 1955 to apply for membership. One was J. B. Pena and the other was Hiram Valdes. J. B. was the superintendent of the San Felipe school district, and Hiram was a civil service worker at Laughlin Air Force Base.

J. B. was one of those few who, through hard work, perseverance, and a bit of good fortune, had received a college education and then returned to educate the kids of San Felipe. He was a slim man and a bit shorter than Hiram. Though in his early forties, he was already showing a receding hair line, which most often he would cover with a stylish fedora.

Hiram had successfully secured a job with the federal government, and though he did not possess the college degree his friend enjoyed, he earned as much. He was fair skinned and sported a flattop haircut and had developed a good golf game while on his first assignment in San Antonio.

They walked into the office of the manager and stood in front of the receptionist. They looked at each other as if to silently determine between the two who would act as the spokesman. J. B. smiled at Hiram and began.

"Young lady, my name is J. B. Pena, and this gentleman is Hiram Valdes. We want to submit our applications for membership," he proudly addressed the young lady.

She gave them a puzzled look and then asked, "You want to do what?"

Without hesitation, J. B. repeated their intentions. "We want to submit our application for membership in the club!"

She looked at them again but said nothing for a moment. "Just one moment," she said as she walked into the manager's office. In a low voice she told her boss, "Mr. Glenn, there are two men out there who say they want to submit their applications for memberships to the club."

"Oh?" he replied with a stirred interest. "Who are they? Did you get their names?"

"Sir, ahh no, but they're Mexican!"

"Ohhh!" He reacted with astonished disbelief.

"What do I do, sir?" she asked.

"Tell them we're not accepting new members right now!" he ordered. "No! Wait. That would be too obvious." He pondered for a moment and then changed his approach. "Go ahead and have them fill out applications and tell them that we will give them to the membership committee for decision."

"Yes, sir," she replied as she started walking back to the men.

"And tell them that the initiation fee is five hundred dollars, if they get approved, that is."

"Yes, sir."

Even though the receptionist had closed the door to the manager's office, J. B. and Hiram could still hear most of what the manager had said. She returned to the reception area and without saying a word, opened a drawer in her desk and pulled out two one-page forms and handed them to the men.

"Fill these out, and we will submit them to the membership committee. Oh and by the way, the membership fee is five hundred dollars. A piece."

"That's not a problem!" J. B. said as he took the forms from her. He then smiled and winked at her. He took a pen from his pocket and began to write the information requested in the form. After finishing, he handed the pen to Hiram, who then filled out his application. Hiram then handed the pen to J. B. along with his form, and J. B. gave the forms and the pen back to the receptionist.

"Here you are, miss. Now when can we expect a decision on these?" he asked.

The receptionist could not think of a word to say, so she got up from her desk and walked back into the manager's office. She returned within seconds and said, "We will let you know as soon as the committee has met."

"But when will that be?" insisted J. B.

"I don't know, sir, but we will let you know." "I see. Well thank you kindly, miss."

J. B. and Hiram walked out of the office, and as soon as the receptionist saw them getting into their car, she ran into the manager's office and handed the applications to her boss.

"Do you want me to put them in an envelope addressed to the membership committee, sir?" she asked.

Looking at the forms, he read the names on them, "J. B. Pena and Hiram Valdes. Hmmm. The committee has already considered them and, sadly, they have been rejected!" he pronounced as he tossed them into his trash can.

"What do I tell them if they come and, you know, ask about their application?"

"Tell them the committee still has not been able to meet to consider their applications."

"Yes, sir."

"Better yet, prepare a letter for my signature saying that the committee is unable to approve their membership at this time. And if they should ask you anything, tell them that's all you know."

"Yes, sir." She walked back to her desk and typed the short letters that would be going to J. B. and Hiram advising them of the rejection of their applications. A thought ran through her head, which made her get up again and go to the manager's office.

"Do you want me to include a reason?"

"Of course not! We don't need to give them a damn reason!" he shouted.

"Yes, sir!" she said as she meekly walked back to her desk.

Two days later, J. B. and Hiram received the letters. Although not surprised, they were disappointed and somewhat hurt. Hiram drove over to J. B.'s house to see if he had also received the same letter. By the time he arrived, J. B. was waiting for him at the door.

"Did you see this?" he asked J. B. as he held the letter in his raised hand and walked closer to J. B.

"Yes, I did," J. B. replied with dejection clearly in his voice.

"How can they deny us membership?" Hiram asked rhetorically.

"We have money to afford the dues! The city owns the land they use for the course, so aren't we the taxpayers who own that land?"

"Yes, you're right Hiram. But they just don't care about that. Let's face it. They don't want us Mexicans as members!"

"But that's not right!" Hiram insisted. "We can play golf! We're not going to harm them or the course!"

"Yes, I know. You're right," J. B. replied with a resigned tone in his voice. "But we can still play. We just have to pay the exorbitant green's fees."

"Yes, but we could save a lot of money if we were members."

"Once again, you're right!" J. B. affirmed.

Hiram shook his head in an effort to contain his anger. A smile ran across his face as a new thought raced in his mind. "There's another reason for my visit," he began. "I wanted to discuss with you an idea I have."

"Oh yeah? What is that?" J. B. asked.

Hiram wasted no time in expressing his idea. "We need to have a high school golf team!" he said boldly.

J. B. was pleasantly surprised upon hearing Hiram's suggestion. "Okay. I'm listening."

"When I was in San Antonio and I was learning the game at the San Pedro driving range, I would see a bunch of young kids who practiced there. I talked to a few of them, and they said they played on their high school golf teams and competed against other schools in tournaments. Don't you think our kids should have that experience?"

"Yes, of course!" J. B. responded. "I don't know how we would do it, but I agree with you!"

"Good! Hiram continued. "So what do we do first?"

"Well," J. B. pondered, "we'll have to present the idea to the school board. But you know the first thing they're going to ask is 'where do we get the money?'"

"Yeah, well, they just need to say yes to the idea. We'll find the money!" Hiram adamantly insisted.

"I like the idea, Hiram! And I know just where we go to get our players!"

They looked and pointed a finger at the other and jointly exclaimed, "The caddies!"

For the next several hours, the two discussed various ideas for how they could convince the school board to allow them to field a high school golf team, along with some notions of raising funds to cover expenses. Although neither was a wealthy man, they were prepared to foot some of the bills for the team themselves. They also talked about how they would go about selecting the players and what problems they would expect to encounter in participating in tournaments, such as actually being permitted to enter some of them. Since J. B. was the superintendent, Hiram pointed out that it was inevitable that J. B. would have to volunteer to serve as the coach, even though Hiram was the better golfer. Hiram would serve as an unofficial and unpaid assistant.

Over the next several weeks, they lobbied each board member to ensure that the idea would be acted upon favorably, a task that challenged every bit of their persuasive skills.

CHAPTER EIGHT

O N A TYPICALLY WARM June morning in 1955, J. B. and Hiram showed up early at the San Felipe Country Club. It was Monday, so they knew that some of the caddies would be playing and no members would be around. They waited by the first tee and before too long, six of the caddies showed up. You wouldn't know it by looking at them, but they were ready to play some golf. They had only two golf bags between them, each of them contained just three or four clubs, and the bags were probably made in the 1930s. They were made of discolored white canvas with scraped brown leather on the top and bottom edges and pockets. The metal used in the straps to carry them, as well as the zippers, had more than their fair share of rust. Nevertheless, the two who carried them did so proudly and were not self-conscious about the bags' appearance. Although some of the boys carried one or two clubs in their hands, they had all agreed that they would share all of the clubs, just as they had done on many previous occasions.

As the caddies approached the first tee, they noticed the two men. The boys knew that they were not members, and they were obviously not there to play golf, as they had no clubs.

"Good morning, boys," J. B. greeted them. "Good morning, sir!" they all replied in unison.

"My name is J. B. Pena, and this is Hiram Valdes. Do you boys mind if we watch you play?"

None of them said anything as they all looked at each other, wondering silently the same thing.

"Why?" Joe broke the silence as the others nodded their heads in agreement with the question they were themselves too shy to ask.

J. B. and Hiram smiled and looked at each other. "Well, we heard some of you were good golfers, and we wanted to see some good golf played."

"We're all good players, mister!" shouted the youngest and smallest, Gene. The rest of the boys started laughing.

"I'm sure you're right, son," J. B. assented.

"No, you were right the first time, mister!" Mario jumped in, halfway joking. "Some of us are good players."

"That's right!" Joe exclaimed as he nudged Gene.

"Well, I'm good for a lefty!" Gene asserted.

"You can watch us if you like," Mario said.

"Yeah, you can watch," Joe confirmed.

"Thank you," Hiram said.

"Let's get going, guys!" Joe said. "I'll go first."

Joe then pulled a nine-iron from the bag, a club with rust spots on both the face and shaft. The rubber grip was worn down by the many times the young hands had gripped the club to propel the golf balls on their way to the green. None of the boys sported the typical golf attire, as all were wearing blue jeans and T-shirts. Despite the hot sun of this June day, none wore caps or other headwear. The tall and lanky Joe took aim at the flag of the green located about 130 yards across the creek and then assumed his stance parallel to the golf ball he had placed on a wooden tee on the grass that was the official tee box. Without anyone telling them to, all the boys suddenly got very quiet as Joe was about to hit. With a long, silky, smooth motion, Joe swung the club back behind him and then quickly reversed the course of the club forward with a speedy momentum that sent the ball on a direct flight path to the flag. Within seconds, the ball landed on the green about five feet from the flag. J. B. and Hiram were obviously impressed; they turned to each other and moved their heads up and down in approval.

"Nice shot, son!" J. B. exclaimed.

"Very good!" Hiram agreed.

"Thank you," Joe replied as he handed the club to Mario.

"Ahhh, he always does that," Gene said matter-of-factly.

Mario then followed with an equally impressive shot, which landed about a foot outside of Joe's ball. Three of the other boys then hit their balls, but only one boy, Felipe, made the green; he was about twenty feet from the hole. The last one to hit was Gene, who was also the youngest. He took the club but did something neither J. B. nor Hiram had seen before. Gene took the club and, even though it was designed for a right-handed player, he laid it on the ground with the back of the face against the ball and took his stance in a mirror image of the boys who had already hit.

"A left-handed stance with a right-handed club?" Hiram whispered to J. B.

With an aggressive swing of the club that kind of chopped down on the ball, Gene struck the ball, but it barely got airborne. The ball hopped down the hill headed toward the creek, but instead of plunging into the water, the ball hit the bridge spanning the creek and bounced over onto the grass situated on the upslope in front of the green."Yesss!" Gene shouted, pleased with his successful aim.

While the other boys were not surprised, having seen this feat on many prior occasions, J. B. and Hiram were visibly shocked. They looked at each other in disbelief and almost broke out in laughter, but they thought better of it. They began walking down the hill following the boys, who were already halfway to the green. As J. B. and Hiram got to the bridge, the boys who had initially missed the green had already hit onto it, except for Gene. J. B. and Hiram moved quickly toward the green. They were interested in seeing three things. They wanted to see Mario and Joe putt their balls to see if they could birdie the holes, and they were anxious to see how Gene would navigate his ball onto the green.

Gene took the same club with which he had hit his first shot and set himself up to the ball. He then bumped the ball, again with the back of the face of the club. It skipped along the grass and then rolled onto the green, landing about ten feet from the cup. This too proved amazing to J. B. and Hiram.

"Ahh, shoot!" Gene uttered, disappointed that his ball did not get closer to the hole. He moved quickly toward the ball, and with a putter that could be used by either a right-handed or a left-handed player, Gene struck the ball toward the hole. To add to his disappointment, the ball rolled past the hole about three inches. He then tapped the ball into the hole, bent over to retrieve it, and handed the putter to Mario, who had already scouted out his line. After assuming his stance next to the ball and glancing three times at the hole, Mario maneuvered the putter toward the ball. With one gentle stroke, the ball began to roll straight to the hole, making the unmistakable sound of a golf ball finding the bottom of cup.

"Ahhlright!" Mario yelled raising his hand. "Match that, Joe!"

"Piece o' cake!" Joe replied with a cocky tone. His confidence was matched only by his skill in getting the ball to the hole. With his well-grooved stroke, the ball followed Mario's into the cup. No need for Joe to show any excitement, as the ball did what he expected.

"Well done, boys!" J. B. expressed his approval.

"Good birdies!" Hiram affirmed.

"Thanks!" was the collective response.

They then moved on to the second hole. Again Joe was the first to hit, having retained the honor by virtue of his birdie. He was followed by Mario, who matched his birdie, and then Felipe, who parred the hole. The other two bogeyed the hole, so they were next, with Gene again being the last one off the tee. He repeated his unusual approach to hitting the ball, sending it hopping down the fairway, but at least it was in play, even though not as long as the rest.

After the players moved on to their balls, with their spectators accompanying them, they waited for Gene to attempt his trick shot again. He lined up the shot and took his backhanded swing of the club at the ball. He made contact, but there was not enough elevation to clear the creek that fronted the second green. Nor did it hit the bridge leading to the green. Instead, after a few bounces, the ball went in for a swim.

"Ohh, no!" the other players cried out.

Dejected, Gene handed the club to Felipe, who was carrying the bag on this hole. The rest managed to hit their balls on the green or on the fringe. Gene, who had walked closer to the creek, dropped a ball to try his luck again. He took a deep breath and swung the club at the ball, making what sounded like good contact. Again the ball barely got off the ground and with no chance to clear the water.

"I'm out of the hole, guys. Just give me an X," Gene said with a disappointed tone in his voice.

"Try another one, Gene!" yelled Joe.

"Nahh, I only have one ball left," Gene replied.

"That's okay, Gene. We'll get the balls after the round," offered Mario.

"Okay! I'll just go to the next hole," Gene said.

J. B. and Hiram had been watching with a shared disappointment, both having made a similar observation. They walked over to Gene, who had crossed the bridge but was heading to the third tee box as the others putted their balls toward the hole.

Hiram expressed his opinions first. "Son, if you're going to play the game, you're going to have to change some things," he began.

Gene looked at him as if to ask what he was talking about.

"I know you're left-handed, but you're going to have to learn to hit the ball right-handed. That's what I did. Do you know what I mean?"

Gene understood exactly what he meant. "I guess so! But I wish they made clubs for guys like me!"

"I understand, son. But I haven't seen any," Hiram replied sympathetically.

"What was your name, son?" J. B. asked. "Gene, sir."

"Gene, give it a try. You should be able to swing from the right just like you do from the left!" J. B. said confidently.

"I'll try," Gene said. As he waited for the other young golfers to finish the second hole, Gene took a club from one of the bags and tried gripping it like a right-hander. They could tell by his expression that the change felt weird to him, but they could also see his determination to swing the club with his weaker side. He took a few swings and quickly realized that it was not going to be as difficult as he had imagined.

"Looks good!" Hiram observed.

"It feels weird," Gene replied. "But I think I can do it!"

"That's the spirit!" chimed in J. B.

By now the others had finished and had apparently caught a glimpse of Gene's effort to change his swing.

"I told you, you should hit right-handed," Mario said, ribbing him.

"Now you'll hit the ball right," Felipe said.

"Only if he swings like me," boasted Joe.

All the boys then laughed in agreement and headed to the third tee box.

They continued playing the balance of the course while J. B. and Hiram observed each of the boys hit impressive shots with shared clubs. They also noticed how even with no golf shoes, their swings were stable and balanced around their slim frames. Some were clearly better than others, but the surprising thing J. B. and Hiram found was that they could actually play the game, the rudimentary equipment notwithstanding.

At the end of the round, J. B. asked the boys if he and Hiram could talk to them as a group.

"About what?" one of them asked.

"We want to talk to you about playing golf as a team," J. B. replied.

The boys mumbled something inaudible among themselves, but before any one of them could ask anything discernible, J. B. continued. "Why don't you boys gather around here, please?" he asked.

As they boys moved around closer to the two observers, J. B. began his sales pitch.

"How would you boys like to play golf on different courses?" he asked.

"Yes, but how?" Mario asked.

"Let him talk," Joe quickly ordered.

"Okay. Okay," Mario obediently backed down.

J. B. smiled in appreciation of the youthful self-disciplining.

"We want to form a golf team for San Felipe High School to compete against other schools," J. B. began. "We're looking for five golfers to make up the team. I think you boys can be those golfers if you'd like."

"Do you have to be in high school to play?" Gene asked eagerly.

"You can't play, Gene! You're still in junior high!" Mario pronounced.

"Yes, son. You have to be in high school," J. B. answered.

"Yeah, and where would we play?" Joe added.

"You would be playing against other high schools in the state and on different courses," J. B. replied.

"We're going to have to see about getting clubs for all of you 'cause you can't play with one bag for all," Hiram pointed out.

"How are we gonna get clubs for all of us?" Felipe asked.

J. B. looked at Hiram, each struggling to come up with a decent response to the legitimate question.

"We'll figure that out," J. B. responded assuringly. "If you guys want to play on our team, we'll take care of that."

"Yeah, we'll handle that for you," Hiram affirmed. "What do you say, boys?" J. B. asked.

The young caddies looked at each other, and Joe was the first to reply.

"I'll play!" he said confidently.

"Yeah. Me too!" Mario joined in.

"I want to play!" added Felipe.

The other two caddies, Alfredo Padilla and Lupe Felan, then voiced their willingness to also participate.

"Gene," J. B. began to say as he turned to the young and disappointed golfer. "You can practice with the team. That way you'll be ready when you go to high school. How 'bout that?"

"All right!" Gene exclaimed. "Thanks."

Joe tousled Gene's hair with his hand and said, "Maybe you'll learn something from us!"

"Yeah! We'll teach you to swing the right way!" Mario added as he and Felipe patted him on the back.

J. B. then collected the necessary information from each of the boys: their names, parents' names, addresses, and so forth.

"We'll let you boys know when we need to start practicing together, but in the meantime, keep working on your swings the way you've been doing. We'll be around to see you play again. Thank you."

"Thank you both," Mario said as he extended his hand to each of the adults. "Thanks for giving us a chance to play for you!"

"Yes. Yes," the rest joined in, expressing their gratitude.

The two adults then walked away, satisfied that their plan was now in motion.

The boys then made their way to their private place to work on their games. They now had a good reason to practice harder at El Llanito Country Club.

CHAPTER NINE

B ETWEEN JUNE AND THE middle of August, J. B. and Hiram would work on a strategy to first equip the new golf team and also arrange to participate in some tournaments against other high schools. They were denied invitations from the predominantly white schools within a two-hours' drive from the city of Del Rio, but they persevered. The first tournament they were fortunate to garner an invitation from was in Edinburg, Texas, which was about seven hours away by car, but that didn't matter to them. It was scheduled for the first week of school, so they knew the boys would have to be pulled from classes for four days. That was not a problem for J. B., who had influence with the high school teachers, and the boys relished the idea of missing school to play golf.

In July, J. B. received a telephone call from the local Coca-Cola distributor, who had learned that he was forming a golf team for the high school. The representative mentioned that the company would be sponsoring a junior competition at the club and asked if any of the boys would like to enter. J. B. assured him that they would, and he thanked him for the offer after getting the details from him.

On the next Monday that the boys were allowed to play at the club, J. B. mentioned the junior tournament to them. Of course, they were all excited and wasted no time in expressing their willingness to enter and play. As they each started to head to the first tee box for their weekly round, Mario noticed that O. B. Poole was waiting by the tee box with a golf bag and a pair of golf shoes in his hand.

Mario was puzzled, as he typically caddied for him during the days that the club was open. "Are you playing today, Mr. Poole?" he asked.

"No, Mario!" he said with a smile on his face. "I'm not playing today, but I figured you would be. I have something for you. I understand you're going to be playing on the high school golf team, so I thought you could use these." He pointed at the clubs in the bag and the golf shoes.

"You're gonna let me use these?" Mario asked with eyes wide open.

"They're yours!" Mr. Poole said. "They're an old extra set I had in my garage, and I no longer use these shoes, so you might as well have them."

"Wow!" Mario exclaimed. "And the bag too?" he asked, shaking with excitement.

"The bag too!" Mr. Poole affirmed.

"Thanks, Mr. Poole! Thank you very much!"

"You're welcome, Mario!"

J. B. approached Mr. Poole and said, "That's mighty nice of you O. B. Thanks." He shook his hand.

"You're welcome, J. B. Let me know if you need anything else."

"Thanks again, O. B.," J. B. repeated.

Mario looked at the contents of the bag. It had a driver, a four-wood, three irons, and a putter. With the seven-iron that Mr. Poole had previously given him, he just about had a full set now. The seven-iron he had gotten before he carried in his hand, but now he had a bag to put it in along with the "new" ones. Now, for the first time, he also had golf shoes, which he quickly tried on. They were a little big, but he figured he could grow into them. For now he would just insert something inside them so that his feet would not slide back and forth during the swing.

While Mario was admiring his new set, Hiram gathered the other boys around a pile of old golf clubs. Some of them had probably not been used for decades, but that didn't matter to the boys.

"Pick out what you think you can use," Hiram directed, but the caddies, now new members of the San Felipe High School Golf Team, had already rummaged through the metal sticks. "We also have some bags you can use," Hiram continued as he pointed at the five old canvas bags on the ground.

Hiram and J. B. had successfully convinced their owners to give them to the boys, but they had forgotten to clean them. They were covered completely with dust, evidence that they had been stored for years with no protection from anything that could cling to them. This also did not matter to the boys. They banged the dust off the bags and inserted the clubs into them. Having golf bags for the first time meant that they would now look like real golfers.

Even Gene was allowed to pick out some of the clubs and a bag. He took advantage of the chance given him to practice with the others. By now he had learned to swing like a "rightie," and his balls were actually getting airborne when he struck them.

"C'mon golfers!" Joe yelled. "Let's get goin'. We got a tournament to win! So let's get ready!"

The boys didn't need any other instruction to get them going to the first tee to begin their practice round. They knew now they had something to play for and there was no time to waste. The six of them took their turns hitting their shots and off they went, with the two spectators in tow.

The following week the boys played in the local Coca-Cola Junior Golf Tournament at San Felipe Country Club. This was the first time the boys had been able to play on the course outside of a Monday. They also had never played with noncaddies, especially white kids.

Joe won the sixteen and up division, while Mario won the fourteen–fifteen group and Felipe came in second. This made J. B. and Hiram excited at the prospects of the beginning of school and their first official competition.

Before the team could participate in any school competitions, the best four players and an alternate had to be chosen. J. B. had arranged one afternoon for the boys to play a round at the club, and the best four scores would determine who would make the trip and who would be the fifth and stay home. Joe, Mario, Felipe, and Lupe made up the first team to compete.

During the first week of September, the new San Felipe Mustang Golf Team headed to Edinburg to participate in their first tournament as a team.

The long drive was exhausting but exciting for the boys, as they had never seen what deep south Texas looked like. They were nervous, since they had competed only once before against other golfers besides themselves. They were all quite familiar with each other's game, but those of the strangers they would battle against presented a unique challenge.

In addition to playing real competitive golf for the first time, the boys faced some conditions they had not experienced before. There were winds unlike the kind found in their home tract. But to their advantage, the fairways were hard, the greens were fast, and the weather was hot and humid. Kind of reminded them of their many rounds at El Llanito.

After a brief practice round on the afternoon of their arrival, the tournament began the next day. J. B. gathered the boys around him just before the first group was to head to the tee. "Boys, have in your mind that this is just another fun round of golf like back home. There's nothing different about this course, so just swing like you always do."

The boys nodded in agreement as they wished each other good luck. "Good luck all!" J. B. added as the boys headed to the first tee.

Each of the boys would be paired with three others with whom they had never played before. This was to guard against any untoward funny business.

In the end, the newness of high school competition proved less than insurmountable for the team. They placed third among the seven schools competing, and Felipe finished as the co-individual medalist along with a player from Mission, just edging out Joe.

Though J. B.'s expectations for his team's success at this first tournament were low, he was pleasantly surprised by the poise of his team members, whose swings had not been subjected to significant tests. The results gave him much satisfaction, and he now felt that organizing the team would be proven to be a wise idea.

CHAPTER TEN

ONCE THE NEW SCHOOL year began, J. B. managed to get the team entered in a tournament in Eagle Pass that included teams from the area and would provide them with a look at the players against whom they would be competing later in the district competition. The schools participating in the tournament were from small cities in and around southwest Texas that did not present any significant competition. The boys finished in first place, running away with it, while Joe, Felipe, and Mario finished in that order in individual play.

The benefit of playing in Eagle Pass was that the boys got valuable tournament competition experience, which they would need if they were to be successful against the better schools in the district and beyond. The success in Eagle Pass was encouraging to all, and it made the boys eager to continue their practice.

A few weeks before the district competition, J. B. told the team members to meet him at the country club right after school let out. This was unusual, as the boys normally caddied in the afternoons. He told them that he had a couple of announcements for them, and they should not be late. Once they all showed up, J. B. gathered them around him.

"Gentlemen," he addressed them. "As you all know, we have the district tournament in two weeks in Crystal City, and I want to make sure that you are ready. I have some good news. Joe Mitchell, whom you know as the pro at San Felipe, has agreed to allow us to practice on the course in the afternoons."

"Ahlright!" blurted out two of the boys, while the rest cheered in appreciation.

"Yes. You should all thank Mr. Mitchell for this. I know you boys do some caddying for the members in the afternoons, but right now I need for you to get in as much practice as you can on a real course."

"El Llanito's a real course, Coach!" shouted Joe, and they all laughed in agreement.

J. B. smiled and said, "I'm sure it is, Joe, but you guys need practice on a course with grass."

When the laughter subsided, J. B. continued. "Now on Saturday, this coming Saturday, we are going to have a practice match with the Del Rio High School golf team ..."

"We seen 'em play," Mario interrupted. "We can kick their butts!" Laughter again followed this bold assertion.

"Yes, well, I need you guys to prove it to some people," J. B. stated.

"What do ya mean, Coach?" Felipe asked.

"Well," he began, pausing for a moment. "This is a new sport for the high school, and I need to show the school board that we deserve the same support that the football and baseball teams get. I want to make sure the school has a golf team for a long time! That's all."

"Yeah, we getcha, Coach," Joe said, expressing his understanding. "We can show 'em."

"Yeah! We can do it, Coach!" The chorus from the boys followed.

"All right, then. Mr. Mitchell is waiting for you boys on the first tee. Have a good practice!" J. B. exclaimed.

With their equipment in tow, the boys quickly made their way to the first tee. Mr. Mitchell greeted them and gave them some admonishments regarding their on-course behavior. He had no doubt that they were all very respectful of the course and were conscious of the proper etiquette, but he was instructed by the club board to make it clear to the boys that playing on the course outside of Mondays was a special privilege, which could be yanked at anytime. Seeing much promise in the boys as golfers, Joe Mitchell had gone to bat for them and was hopeful that their success would dispel the skepticism expressed by the members.

The boys had already developed a liking to him, ever since he had organized the caddies and provided some structure. Instead of allowing them to run to the parking lot each time they sought a caddying job, he had established a classification system that would help the members know who was indeed capable of providing top-notch caddying. Once he observed the boys in their caddying roles and spoke to the members about each of them, he selected the more experienced ones to be Class A caddies, and these were the ones requested most often by the players. The new ones who had not yet caddied or had had a few jobs but were still learning were deemed Class C caddies. Those in between were considered Class B caddies. All of the members of this team had earned their Class A status. None of them had any reason to question Mr. Mitchell's fairness in the selection process, as he had established credibility with the boys.

Once Mr. Mitchell finished his instructions, he noticed Gene among the boys, and he had his bag and clubs. So, he asked him, "Gene, you a member of this team?"

"No, sir," he politely replied. "But Coach told me I could practice with the team 'cause I'm gonna be on the team next year."

Mr. Mitchell looked at J. B., who nodded affirmatively to confirm Gene's assertion. "Okay, son. You can play with them."

"Thank you, sir!" Gene said as he quickly lined up behind the others so that he too could hit his golf ball off the tee.

In their blue jeans and T-shirts, they proceeded to play their practice round.

Though he was officially the coach, there was not much J. B. could offer in the way of swing analysis or adjustments beyond his words of encouragement. He had not developed or improved his own golf game, but he truly had the golf bug in him. Hiram was a better player and could offer the boys some tips, but they were primarily left to their own volition to improve their swings and overall game. It was the boys' instincts and their observations of the players for whom they looped that provided the best instruction. They had also spent hours reading some of the golf magazines they found in the trash, which had been thrown away by some club members.

CHAPTER ELEVEN

O N THAT FOLLOWING SATURDAY morning, the young Mustang team arrived on the course ready to take on their Wildcat counterparts. The Del Rio High School golf team did not compete in the same scholastic level, as it belonged to Class A, while the Mustangs were B. The Del Rio school was bigger and had a greater enrollment. So this was a first for the boys, and it sent a weirdness through their minds, as they had from time to time caddied for the same golfers against whom they were now going to compete.

When Mario had expressed confidence that they could defeat their crosstown opponents, it was not a blind and careless observation, for he had seen the swings of the white rivals. He and the others were well acquainted with the capabilities of the group.

The four who would be competing against the sons of club members were Joe, Mario, Felipe, and Lupe. Gene would not be playing, but there was no way he was going to miss seeing his close friends take on the privileged kids. While they waited for J. B. and the Del Rio coach, as well as one of the boys from the Wildcat team, the Mustang team members sat quietly on the ground by the first tee. They had said "hello" to the three Wildcats who were there but not much more. The three Wildcats acted as if they were the only ones there and engaged in typical boyish horseplay. They referred to each other in derogatory terms and punched one another on the arms, often criticizing their golf swings and claiming that their teammates could not "break a hundred." Joe and his fellow teammates observed them but made no comments even as the three miscreants ran through where the boys were sitting.

Finally, J. B. and the Del Rio coach arrived and exchanged pleasantries. They discussed how they were going to handle the competition, and upon agreeing on something, J. B. came to address his players.

"All right, boys. Gather round."

The boys quickly got on their feet and assembled in front of him.

J. B. continued, "Two of you are going to play with two of their players, and the other two of you with the other of their two. So Joe and Felipe will go with the first group, and Mario and Lupe the second group. Any questions?"

"No, sir," they replied in unison.

"Very well, then. Let's get going," J. B. instructed.

The Del Rio coach stepped up to the first tee and said, "J. B., since your boys are the guests, they can tee off first."

"Thank you, Coach," J. B. replied.

"Lead us off, Joe!" J. B. instructed, and Joe wasted no time in getting his club and teeing up the ball to begin the competition. In response to a fluid, well-timed swing, the ball sailed into the air straight in the direction of the green. When it landed, it stopped about six feet away from the flag.

"Good shot, son!" the Del Rio coach observed out loud.

"Thank you, sir!" Joe acknowledged.

The two Del Rio boys looked at each other but said nothing. Felipe was next to hit. It was almost an instant replay of the first strike, as his ball landed almost the same distance from the hole but on the opposite side of Joe's.

"That's another good shot, son!" the Del Rio coach repeated.

"Thank you, sir." Felipe responded. Again the two Wildcats looked at each other, but this time one of them made a comment that didn't make his coach very proud.

"We're so fucked!" he said as he prepared to make his swing and then managed to try to fulfill his own prophecy. His shot flew to the right of the green and landed in the sand bunker situated next to it. As his partner saw this, he cleared his throat and then made a nervous effort to improve on his teammate's bad result. He barely managed to clear the creek, and his ball landed quite short of the green. Joe and Felipe gathered their bags and, without saying a word, quickly walked down toward the bridge that would allow them passage to the friendly green.

The other two in their foursome grumbled at each other and showed a lack of the poise they saw in their opponents.

Felipe and Joe waited patiently as the others whacked their way onto the green. The one short of the green skulled his shot over the opposite side of the green, and the one in the sand took two swings to extricate his ball from the bunker. By the time the four finished the hole, two double bogeys by the Wildcats bowed humbly to the birdies by the Mustangs. Hiram, whom J. B. had asked to follow the first group while he went with the second, smiled and nodded his approval.

"Good birdies, guys!" said one of the other Wildcats as they headed to the second hole.

"Thanks!" Joe replied.

"Yeah, thanks!" Felipe said.

It was then the second group's turn to begin play. Out of these four, only Mario managed to place his ball on the green, resulting in a par, while the other three bogeyed to start their rounds.

This pattern repeated itself throughout the round, as the Del Rio players never were able to get control over their shots. By the time the round was over, the Mustangs had demonstrated their superior skills and talent for the game. Even though the Del Rio boys enjoyed more time on the course and had the benefit of professional lessons paid for by their fathers, they were obviously outmatched by the smaller-school players.

After they had exchanged their customary pleasantries on the eighteenth green, the players from both teams thanked their coach and Mr. Mitchell for arranging the match. The boys then began their walks home. Two of the Del Rio boys were walking by Felipe when one of them expressed his analysis of their failure that day.

"You know why they beat us today?" he asked his teammate but didn't give him a chance to answer. "'Cause we're not disciplined like them, and we don't take things seriously like they do!"

The other boy didn't know what to say as he pondered whether to agree with his friend or not. Before he could comment, the first one followed up on his own assessment.

"Nah!" he exclaimed. "It's cause we have no fucking talent! That's it!" They both laughed heartily as they walked passed Felipe. "See you later, Phil," one of them said.

Felipe was stunned and couldn't believe what he had heard.

Nobody had assessed things that way, and he had never heard anything complimentary from the golfers with privileges.

"Okay. See ya!" Felipe uttered. He then waited for his teammates to catch up to him. "Did you guys hear what they said?" he asked them.

"No, what they say?" Mario asked.

Felipe then proceeded to relay the comments made within his earshot. They all laughed when Felipe repeated the words used by the Del Rio player.

"What are we gonna do now?" Joe asked.

"I wanna play!" Gene cried out.

"Yeah, let's go play some more. It's still light out!" observed Mario. "Yeah!" they all agreed.

With that, they headed to their own little sanctuary, their handmade exclusive course, El Llanito Country Club, for their own brand of respite.

CHAPTER TWELVE

AFTER SOME SUCCESSFUL STINTS of competitive golf, the Mustang golf team was now ready for the 1956 district tournament for Class B schools in Crystal City, Texas. The boys had never played the municipal course before, so J. B. decided to take them a day early so that they could get in a practice round. As with all other trips, J. B. drove the boys in his 1955 Pontiac Star Chief with its shiny red paint on the bottom and a white top. Riding in this car made the trip bearable, even if four of the boys had to crowd into the back seat, while one of them sat between Hiram and J. B., who enjoyed the front.

They arrived at the Crystal City Municipal Golf Course on the Tuesday before the Wednesday through Thursday tournament began, happy that they would be missing school for most of the week. It was a busy day at the course as most, if not all, of the participating schools had also come to practice. Making room for all of the players on this nine-hole course was going to be difficult. Fortunately, J. B. had called ahead and had reserved two tee times in the afternoon for his team.

"We tee off at one and one ten, fellas, so let's go warm up," J. B. said.

"Sure thing, Coach!" replied Joe as the boys unloaded their golf equipment from the spacious trunk.

"What time is it now, Coach?" Mario asked.

J. B. looked at his watch and responded, "It's ten till twelve, so we have just enough time to hit some balls and get ready."

"Okay. Thanks, Coach," Mario said.

With their bags hanging from their young shoulders, the Mustangs headed toward the practice tees. Upon arriving at the hitting area, the boys glanced down at the ground and saw other players hitting golf balls off mats made from old cut-up rubber tires held together by wires.

"What is that, Coach?" Joe asked.

Puzzled and surprised, J. B. looked at Hiram and asked, "You ever seen anything like this, Hiram?"

"No," he replied. "I guess they don't have any grass to hit from."

"Well it can't be any worse than hitting off hard ground," Mario observed.

"That's for sure," Joe chimed in.

Felipe smiled and added, "I hope they don't have those things on the real tee boxes!"

"Surely they wouldn't," J. B. wondered out loud.

"Well, everyone is gonna have to hit from them if they do, so it shouldn't be a problem," Hiram pointed out.

The boys each found a place to begin their practice and started hitting some iron shots from the mats after observing some of the others who had arrived before them. They noticed that the clubs bounced off the mats on each strike, causing thin shots if the ball was not struck first.

"It's like hitting off hard ground," Mario explained. "So you have to pick the ball clean so you won't catch it thin." He then demonstrated his theory with a swing he had learned at El Llanito, where there was no grass to hit from. He recalled that if the club hit the ground before the ball, it would bounce up just enough to strike the upper part of the ball and send it flying low and hot. Mario set up to the ball and swung the club along a path that caused the face to hit the ball without making any significant contact with the mat. The ball sailed straight into the sky, never deviating either left or right.

"I can do that too!" yelled Joe and began to demonstrate with his swing, which produced a very similar result.

"Me too!" followed Felipe. "Just like we did at El Llanito."

The fourth member of the team, Lupe, tried a few swings before he could get the hang of it. Some would fly straight, but many were going low and to the right. This tendency would prove challenging during actual competition.

When they arrived at the first tee box at their appointed time, they discovered that the same type of mat was being used on the tee boxes.

The starter explained to J. B. that they had experienced a difficult time growing grass on the tee boxes but assured him that the rest of the course was in good condition and no mats would be necessary there.

All the players used the mat and began their practice round with no complaints. Playing each hole twice on this nine-hole course gave them the chance to become quite familiar with the layout. By the time the actual tournament began the next day, the new course reminded them of, not only the club back at San Felipe, but their times at El Llanito as well.

By the end of the round, the boys had managed to win the district title going away. Felipe's seventy-five earned him individual medalist honors, with Joe placing second, and Mario third. Lupe did not play as well, but his score did nothing to deprive the team of the best four-man total. After the winners were recognized, J. B. assembled the boys near the car.

"That was a fine display of golf by all of you, and it is a very nice victory for San Felipe. This is our first district title, and I'm sure everyone back home will be very proud of you, just like me. But this is just the beginning! We now have to go to San Marcos for the regional championship in two weeks!"

"Ahh, we can win that one too, Coach!" exclaimed Mario with youthful bravado.

"Piece o' cake," added Joe, and they all laughed.

"Well, let's not count our chickens yet, boys," J. B. warned. "The teams we'll face will be better than those today. You can count on that!"

"We can take 'em, Coach!" Felipe said, joining the confidence blast.

"I'm sure you can, but we're going to go back home and get ready anyway! All right?"

"Sure thing, Coach, but can we get something to eat before we leave?" Joe asked, and the rest of them agreed on the need for food.

"I suppose we can stop someplace and do that," J. B. replied. "What do you think, Hiram?"

"Yeah, let's do that. I know a place near here where they have good burgers," Hiram responded.

They all climbed into the Pontiac and left the course as district champions.

CHAPTER THIRTEEN

The two weeks they had to get ready for the regional tournament seemed to drag on forever, as they were all anxious to travel to San Marcos and show everyone that they could do what they had boasted of being capable of to their coach. After additional practice on their home course, the San Felipe Mustang Golf Team members arrived at the Texas State Teachers College Golf Course ready to take on the other winners of their respective districts. They arrived in J. B.'s red-and-white Pontiac following the four-hour drive they had begun at four in the morning, but they were not too tired.

"Let's get ready for our tee times, boys," J. B. instructed. "We have less than an hour before the first group tees off."

The boys silently but quickly gathered their equipment and headed for the practice range. They knew the type of shots they would have to make to shoot a good score, and they had practiced them back home. They felt ready and confident and could not wait to get on the course.

Joe was the first of them to begin the round, along with three strangers. He should have felt intimidated seeing the unknown white players, but for some reason, the others seemed intrigued by him. He politely greeted them as they introduced themselves to him, and then he proceeded to stripe his shot down the middle of the fairway. He didn't even wait for the ball to land, as he knew already that it had been perfectly struck. He bent over to retrieve the tee from the ground, picked up his bag to return the club to its resting place, and moved to the side to allow the others to hit. He looked back at his teammates, who were waiting to begin their rounds, and winked at them. They smiled and nodded in approval while J. B. and Hiram voiced their pleasure.

"Good shot, Joe," they said. Joe smiled at them and then walked away.

The round for him proved to be steady and reliable. His swing held up for the eighteen holes, the score for which would be combined with those of his teammates for the total that would be matched against the other schools.

Felipe would join the second group that began play, followed by Lupe, and then Mario in the fourth group. There were four schools competing, and only one of them would advance to the state championship in Austin. Though the boys knew they should not be thinking ahead, they felt that they could win and they had told J. B. and Hiram to make plans for the trip to the capitol.

J. B. and Hiram anxiously waited for each of the groups to come to the scorer's tent following completion of the rounds. They saw when Joe came in and turned in his card. Once the man at the table checked out the scores, Joe walked over to his coach with a slow and foot dragging gait that signaled disappointment.

"How'd you do, Joe?" J. B. asked.

"Okay, I guess," he replied. "Seventy-five."

"Not bad, son," J. B. said encouragingly.

"What did the others in your group shoot, Joe?" asked Hiram. "Ahh, eighty, eighty-one, and ninety-one, I believe," Joe answered.

"Well, that means we're in the lead, so you did great, Joe," J. B. congratulated him.

"Thanks, Coach," Joe said, finally smiling.

After about twenty minutes, the second group came in. Felipe seemed more upbeat, as he had a smile across his face. He made his way to the scorer's table and handed in his card after another boy signed it.

"Nice playing with you, Phil," the boy said to Felipe and walked away. "Thanks," Felipe replied. "Good playing with you too!"

As soon as the man signaled to him that his card had been accepted, Felipe ran over to where Joe, J. B., and Hiram were gathered.

Before J. B. asked him, Felipe blurted out, "I shot a seventy-four, Coach!"

J. B. looked at Hiram and smiled. "That's great, Felipe!"

Joe patted Felipe on the shoulder and said, *"Te aventaste,* Phil!"

Hiram shook Felipe's hand and said, "Nice play, Felipe! Well done!"

"What did the others shoot?" J. B. asked anxiously.

"There was a seventy-nine and two eighty-sixes," he replied.

"Oh yes!" J. B. exclaimed as he pumped his fist. "We're still in the lead!"

A short while later, Lupe's group came in, and the San Felipe clan went to greet him. His eighty-one was disappointing, but the score didn't diminish the lead they had accumulated to this point, despite the scores of the members of Lupe's group, which included a seventy-eight, an eighty, and an eighty-two.

Now only one group remained, and J. B. and Hiram as well as the boys knew that unless Mario had totally fallen apart, they were going to make the trip to the state championship in this, their first year of competition.

From a short distance they all waited for Mario to come in. As they saw him approaching the scorer's table, Joe held out his arms palms up to signal to Mario the question of the day. Mario saw him, but all he did was smile. Joe repeated his hand-gestured question to no avail. Mario just walked over to the table and waited for the man to accept his card. No sooner had the man done so than Mario ran toward them.

"A seventy-seven!" he shouted as he was greeted by the team with pats on the head and arms.

After quickly doing the math calculations in his head, J. B. again looked at Hiram and said, "We did it, fellas! We're going to state!"

While the results had not been officially declared, J. B. and the boys knew that the final total of the scores would show that they had won the regional tournament and would next be traveling to Austin. They hugged each other and laughed excitedly. Their predictions had proven true.

"I told you we'd do it, Coach!" Mario exclaimed.

"Yeah, Coach! We told ya!" Joe followed.

"Yes, you certainly did," J. B. replied.

Before long the official results were posted and announced to all. San Felipe High School was the regional champion of golf for 1956 and would now advance to the state championship in Austin. Felipe was announced as the individual regional medalist, while Joe came in second and Mario third. They had come a long way in such a short time, but the real test was coming.

CHAPTER FOURTEEN

"Do you think we'll ever stop playing El Llanito?" Mario asked Joe as they hauled their golf bags around the course they had created.

"Why should we?" Joe responded with his own question.

"Yeah, why would we stop?" asked Gene, who tagged along during their practice.

"I don't know," Mario said as he tried to come up with an explanation. "I guess 'cause we can now practice at the club, so I figure, maybe we don't need this place."

Joe pondered for a while and then responded, "Yeah, but nobody can tell us anything here!"

"Yeah, we can do whatever we want to here!" Felipe added.

Mario thought about it for a while and then nodded his head in agreement. "I guess you're right."

"He sure is!" Gene chimed in. "This is our place! No one can tell us anything!"

Everyone laughed, not only because of the boldness of Gene's innocent statement, but because they all understood that even though they were allowed to practice at the country club, it was a place where they did not belong. El Llanito, on the other hand, was home, their home.

"Do you think we have any chance to win state, Joe?" Felipe asked.

Joe tried to express confidence, but he had a little trouble vocalizing a response. "Sure we do!" he said but not quite convincingly.

"Are you scared?" Felipe asked. "Nahh!" was his quick reply. "Are you?"

Felipe shook his head from side to side but did not utter a word.

"Best way not to get scared is to practice more than the other guys!" Mario philosophized out loud.

"Well we better practice, then," Joe said with stoic resignation.

A week later they were in Austin for the first time in their lives. They had arrived late in the evening before the first round because of some problems with J. B.'s car, which delayed their departure. As a result, they were unable to get a practice round in. They would just have to become acquainted with the fairways and greens of the Austin Country Club as they played each hole. For this, they would be at a disadvantage going against schools that had arrived the day before and had the opportunity to play a practice round. Six schools in their division were vying for the top crown, while thirty players were after the individual title.

J. B. and Hiram had selected a motel just off the highway into Austin. All except Lupe and Felipe had gone inside their room with their luggage. As Lupe removed his bag from the trunk, he closed the lid without thinking.

"Hey don't close it yet!" Felipe shouted, but it was too late. "I haven't got my bag out."

"Oh shit! Sorry," Lupe exclaimed. He put his hand in his pocket in an attempt to retrieve the key to the trunk, but there was nothing there.

"Oh no!" he cried out. "I left the key in the trunk!"

"Ahh, *que tonto!*" said Felipe. "What do we do now?"

"Maybe Coach has another key," suggested Lupe. "Well, go ask him!" Felipe ordered.

"I don't wanna ask him. He'll get mad at me!"

"Well, he should! You're the one who left them in the trunk!"

"Hell, I don't want to! What else can we do?" Lupe pleaded.

Just as Lupe was struggling with the notion that he would have to embarrass himself with the coach and the other players if he told them what he did, Felipe noticed another man unloading his luggage from his car, which was parked a few stalls away.

"I've got an idea!" Felipe said as he walked over to the man. "Excuse me, mister," he said.

The man turned and looked at him without saying anything.

"My friend locked the keys inside the trunk of our car. Could we borrow your key, please?"

The man had a puzzled look on his face and replied, "I don't think that will work, son, but you can try." The man handed him the keys and watched as Felipe walked back to J. B.'s car. The man's vehicle was also a Pontiac, so Felipe wasn't too far off in thinking that his idea would work. He picked the key that resembled the one to J. B.'s car, inserted it in the trunk's keyhole and turned it. To their surprise, the trunk lid opened, and a huge smile ran across both boys' faces. Felipe pulled the key from the hole and walked over to the man.

"Thank you, sir!" he said as he handed him the keys.

"I don't believe it!" the man said. "I've seen everything now!" he exclaimed. "You're welcome, son."

When Felipe returned to J. B.'s car, Lupe had already pulled Felipe's bag out of the trunk and held the keys in his hand.

"Can I close it now?" he asked Felipe.

"Yeah, but don't think I won't tell Coach what you did!"

"Ahh, c'mon Phil!" Lupe pleaded. "Don't tell 'em."

Felipe laughed and ran toward the room as Lupe tried to catch up with him.

The following day, the boys were ready for the most challenging tournament of their young lives. They arrived at the course with little clue as to what to expect but with the confidence that they had built up from the successes leading up to it.

J. B. gathered the team around him by the car before they headed for the practice tee and tried to give them some words of encouragement.

"Boys, I know you won the district and the regional without much trouble, but at this point you will be competing against the best golfers in the state!"

"But, Coach," Joe began to point out, "since we're here, doesn't that mean that we are some of the best golfers in the state?"

"Yeah! That's right!" the others joined in.

J. B. looked at Hiram, and they both began laughing.

"Yes, Joe. You're right." J. B. said. "But what I'm trying to say is that this is going to be the toughest competition you have ever faced, so it won't be easy. Play like you would if you were back at San Felipe. You will all have to play your best to have any chance of winning! You boys may hear some derogatory comments from some of the other players, but I want you to remember not to react in any way that will get you in trouble and disqualified."

"We'll do our best, Coach!" Mario said. "Just like we always do!"

"Yeah, Coach!" they all chimed in. "We'll give it our best!"

"All right, then. Let's go do it!"

That first day of the tournament, the boys appeared relaxed and confident when they showed up at the practice range. Several other boys were practicing their swings when the Mustangs walked up with their golf bags. The others turned to them and stopped hitting balls. They stared at the kids with blue jeans and T-shirts and their old canvas golf bags and started laughing and pointing at them.

"Who are you guys?" shouted one of the other players.

"What makes you think you belong here?" asked another with disdain in his voice.

"Yeah! No Meskins play golf!" another crowed. "So what are you doing here?"

Mario, Joe, Felipe, and Lupe looked at each other and remembered that J. B. had told them that no matter what anyone said or did to them, they had to maintain their composure and do nothing that would get them disqualified.

"We're from San Felipe High School," Mario finally responded. "Where's that?" one tall kid with short blonde hair asked.

"It's in Del Rio," Joe replied.

"Don't know where that is either," the kid claimed.

Two of the other boys had walked closer to Mario and the rest and were looking closely at the old rusted clubs in the bags with the worn grips. One of the boys pulled out an iron and upon noticing its condition, began laughing and asked, "How can you play with this crap?"

The Mustangs were embarrassed as they looked at the others' clubs, seeing the vast difference in the style and quality of the equipment compared to theirs.

"We do just fine!" Mario fired back. "We got here, didn't we?" "C'mon guys!" Joe directed his teammates. "Let's hit balls!"

The Mustangs made their way to the practice tee with their bags as the others continued their demeaning laughter. Despite the mocking by the other players, the boys refused to allow anything to detract from their confidence, and their practice swings reflected it. As they hit ball after ball with their outdated equipment, a couple of the other players stopped to watch them. They said nothing, but the look in their eyes reflected their amazement and surprise as they saw the balls flying high, straight, and long when Joe and his teammates struck them. They could not believe that the Mustangs were doing that with the clubs they were using. They shook their heads and returned to practicing themselves.

Following the practice, the boys teed off one by one. Although their warm-up reflected smooth and confident swings, they did not play extremely well, but they kept up with the competitors in their own group. At the end of the day, San Felipe posted a total team score of 328, but this put them in second place to Ranger's total of 322, just six strokes down.

The next day they arrived at the course feeling positive about their chances of catching up and overcoming their main opponent. Once they gathered their equipment, they headed to the practice area and warmed up. After a few moments, Joe was called up to the first tee, where he would meet his three competitors for the first time. Once they introduced each other and exchanged scorecards, it was time for Joe to hit his tee shot. As he stood on the box, he began feeling a little different. He was actually a bit nervous and looked back to try to see his teammates but could not. He did not know why he did so, but something made him want to look for some help. He took a deep breath and let the club fly. The ball took off but was slightly off course. He pulled it left, but it was still in play as it came to rest in the rough close to one of the trees that lined the fairway. "Good," he thought. "I don't have to hit another one."

He waited for the other players to hit their shots and then picked up his bag and began walking. He hadn't even noticed where their balls had landed, and he really wasn't concerned about them. He just wanted to get to his ball so he could hit it like he knew how. His aim was to convince himself that he really was not nervous and would show his opponents that he could play.

After the first group had cleared the fairway, Mario was the next Mustang golfer to be called to the tee. He too experienced that same weird feeling of nervousness, which had not appeared in the previous tournaments. He shook his hands and arms and took some deep breaths and then began his pre-shot routine. He looked down the fairway and closed his eyes to see his ball flying straight out there in his mind. He then looked down at his ball and gave it a whack. The sound it made told him instantly that he had not hit it purely. It went straight, but because he hit it with the bottom portion of the clubhead, it did not get up very high and did not travel as far as the others.

Once the second group had cleared the teeing area, Lupe was next, and he too experienced some difficulty getting off the tee box. He pushed his shot to the right and hit a tree situated around 50 yards in front of the box but kicked back onto the fairway. It was not the kind of start he was hoping for, but he kept the frustration to himself and just walked quietly toward his ball.

Following the third foursome, it was Felipe's turn. J. B. looked at him anxiously, as he had already witnessed a shaky start from his team. As Felipe took his swing, J. B. gritted his teeth and then saw that the ball was in the air on a decent trajectory, but the look on Felipe's face indicated that he too was unhappy with his first shot. It started on a path down the fairway but drew a little too much and landed in the rough. J. B. sensed the difference in his boys that day. He chalked it up to nerves but felt confident that once they got the first hole out of the way, they would relax and do better. For the most part, this proved to be true, but not entirely.

J. B. decided to go catch up to Joe's foursome to see if Joe had settled down and was playing better. By the time he caught up to him at the ninth hole, Joe was coming off the green. The look on his face said it all.

"How's it going Joe?" J. B. asked.

"Just double-bogeyed the hole, Coach," Joe said with disappointment all across his face and in his voice. "Shot forty-two!"

"That's okay, son!" J. B. tried to console him and be encouraging. "You still have nine holes to go. You can get it back on track. I know you can do it, and you know you can do it!"

"I'll do my best, Coach!" Joe replied as he walked briskly to the tenth tee, not even wanting to take a break and stop at the concession booth. When he arrived at the tenth tee, he waited for the others to get there, as they had decided to stop momentarily. He knew he couldn't hit his ball yet, as he did not have honors after his score on the ninth.

J. B. decided to wait for the other groups by the ninth green so that he could see what each had scored for the first nine holes and determine where the team stood at the halfway point. Mario was the next to hole out on number nine.

"How are you doing, Mario? J. B. asked.

"I've had better days, Coach!" he said with a slight anger in his voice. "I broke my putter on the fourth hole!"

"What happened?" the shocked J. B. asked.

"I kicked it when I missed the putt, and the shaft split in two!" Mario explained.

J. B. shook his head in disapproval. "That temper of yours in going to get you DQd! So what are you using to putt, son?"

"My driver," Mario embarrassingly replied. "But it's working okay."

"Well, I'll get you a backup putter from the car," J. B. offered.

"No, Coach! You can't do that or I'll really get disqualified!" Mario warned.

"Oh, you're right. Well, do the best you can with your driver," J. B. urged. "What's your score for the front?"

"I'm at forty-one."

"Well, that's not too bad, son," J. B. tried to reassure him. "You can make up some ground on the back nine!"

"I suppose," Mario replied with a lack of confidence in his voice and then realized his poor attitude. "Yeah! You're right, Coach. I can do it!"

"That's what I want to hear!" J. B. urged as Mario walked with the others to the tenth tee.

When Lupe came to the ninth green and putted out, J. B. was still there waiting. The news was also discouraging, as Lupe reported a forty-five as his score on the first nine. However, when he obtained the scores for the players from the other schools at the halfway mark, it did not look as bleak as he had assumed. Despite his team's weak start, the Ranger team was only a handful of strokes ahead of the Mustangs. They certainly were not showing that they were going to run away with the trophy.

A bit of bright news came when Felipe made the turn. He had managed to keep his score under forty, although at thirty-nine, it was not looking like the stellar round that could put his team ahead, but it kept them close. Everyone would have to make a surge, or the first trip to the state tournament would be a disappointment.

As J. B. looked at his tally sheet, he shook his head and turned to Hiram. "We're now eight strokes down to Ranger. You think we can make them up on the back?"

Hiram thought for a moment and hesitatingly admitted, "That's going to be hard to do, J. B."

"I know," he said. "I think you're right."

"Let's catch them at the eighteenth," Hiram suggested, and they both headed that way.

Joe had been able to control his swing better on the back but kept being frustrated by his inability to sink the birdie putts. He had bogeyed one of the holes and going to eighteen, he had a chance to get his first birdie and shoot an even par for the back. J. B. and Hiram caught up with him as he was sizing up his putt. Joe calmly looked at his ball and the hole from every angle and then stood by his ball ready for the putt. If he could make this one birdie, in his mind it would make the bad round easier to accept. Alas, it was not to be. After he stroked the ball, it looked like it was headed right for the hole, but it seemed like it hit a slight bump on the green, causing it to turn slightly left of the hole. The ball still caught the left edge of the hole, but it rolled around it and stopped on the right side, just one inch away, prompting audible groans from J. B. and Hiram. Joe quickly tapped it in, pulled the ball from the hole, and then tried to shake the hands of his fellow competitors, but they turned and walked away without acknowledging him. As he walked over to J. B. and Hiram shaking his head in disbelief, he summed up his round.

"Just couldn't get it going today, Coach," Joe said as he showed them the improved score on the back nine, a thirty-seven.

"Well," Hiram said, "that's a seventy-nine, so not bad, Joe."

"I guess, but the kid from Ranger shot a seventy-three, and I know I could've beat him, but my putts just weren't falling," Joe said.

"You did just fine, Joe!" J. B. said encouragingly. "You never know what the total will be until the last player comes in." Privately, J. B. knew their chances were now bleaker, as he recognized Joe was his best player. It would take a miracle to overcome the deficit created by the first Ranger score posted. He was hopeful but prepared to accept bad news.

The group with Mario came to the eighteenth green as J. B. was writing down the scores of the other players in Joe's group. He tried to read Mario's face, but Mario never turned in their direction. When he made the last stroke by putting his ball into the hole, he politely congratulated his playing companions and then headed toward Joe. The tears in his eyes told Joe that Mario too had suffered through a bad round.

"How'd you do? Joe asked.

"A lousy eighty-two!" Mario replied as he fought to keep from crying out loud.

"That's not bad," Joe insisted as he put his arm around him. "It was a tough course, and a lot of the guys played crappy."

"Oh yeah?" Mario asked incredulously. "What you shoot?"

"A seventy-nine," Joe said, embarrassed.

"Really?" Mario asked in disbelief. "Man, you sucked today!"

"Hey! Watch it!" Joe protested, but in his mind he was relieved to see that Mario's sense of humor came through and he would not see any tears from him now. He laughed and pretended to choke Mario for making the disparaging remark.

Upon hearing Mario's score and getting the scores of the other players in his group, J. B. became quite nervous and was now looking for his last two players to make a great showing or else Ranger would be poised to claim the state trophy.

Lupe and his group next made their way to the last hole of the tournament. The way he was walking with his shoulders dropped and his head down was all the indication J. B. needed to acknowledge the inevitable. Lupe had matched his front nine score with an identical one for the back, giving him a total of ninety. J. B. now knew that the only way for the Mustangs to overcome the gap established by the Ranger players was for Felipe to come in with a strong score on the back nine holes, and the Ranger player with a forty-seven or higher for his back nine score.

By the time that Felipe and his group reached the final hole, the fate had already been sealed. Felipe's seventy-eight was an impressive score, considering the circumstances, and though the Ranger player shot an eighty-five, it was enough to add to the success of his team. Ranger managed to take the tournament by a mere three strokes. That left the Mustangs at a close second place, but it might as well have been a hundred strokes, as the boys weren't thinking about anything other than first.

Although disappointed, J. B. wanted his boys to understand that they had come a long way from the caddying days at San Felipe Country Club. After the presentations were made to the winners, J. B. gathered his team by his car.

"Boys, I know you're all disappointed 'cause we didn't win today, but I'm very proud of you for having come this far. It seems like just days ago that you were caddies in a game many said we don't belong in. You have shown everyone that you can play with the best of them, and you have nothing to feel ashamed of. We'll get another chance next year if you guys are willing to work harder and not give up. Are you with me?"

"Yeah! Coach! We're with you!" they all replied with confidence. "We'll come back and kick some butt next year!" Mario announced. "Damn right!" Joe followed.

"Right! That's right!" Felipe and Lupe shouted in agreement.

"We played like crap and only lost by three strokes," Joe observed. "We can win this thing if we play like we know we can!"

"Well, then. Let's go get a good dinner and then we head for home," J. B. said.

After hearing the encouraging words from J. B. and the boys, Hiram walked over to say good-bye to one of the coaches he had met at the tournament and who had invited the team to participate in his school's tournament next season. Once he had done so, he walked by one of the officials from the Texas Interscholastic League, who was talking to the Ranger coach.

"I'm sure glad your team took the tournament, Coach," the official said within Hiram's earshot. "I would have hated to hand that trophy over to them Mexican boys!"

That last comment made Hiram stop in his tracks. He noticed that the Ranger coach had seen him as the official made the comment. The coach quickly said "thanks" and walked away, not wanting to give Hiram the impression that he shared the sentiments of the official, who had not yet seen Hiram.

"We'll be back next year!" Hiram assured the official. "Be waiting for us!"

The official's face turned red, but he couldn't manage to say anything in response before Hiram walked away.

CHAPTER FIFTEEN

AFTER HAVING TASTED THE sweetness that comes from successful competitive golf, the boys settled back into their roles as caddies, but with a new attitude. They had experienced the joy of defeating golfers who had enjoyed a more privileged upbringing. They understood that even though they had fallen one step short of the top prize, they could hang with the best young golfers in the state. They now had the fire in their belly and could not wait to make another trip to Austin, but they were realistic and understood that the trip to the championship required starting at the beginning once again. It would be more challenging now that San Felipe had been classified as a Class A high school due to an increase in the school's enrollment.

During the fall of 1956, the four members of the second-place Mustang golf team were joined by little Gene Vasquez, who was now a freshman at the high school. After school was out, the five—Joe Trevino, Mario Lomas, Lupe Felan, Felipe Romero, and Gene—would rush over to the San Felipe Country Club and take on a looping job for some of the members. After the round, they headed straight for their own place at El Llanito to practice until darkness made them stop. On Mondays they continued to play at the country club, just as the pro had allowed them to do when they were just caddies. This continued throughout the months leading into the spring of 1957. Now that they were competitors, they were welcomed by the members, or at least most of them, on the days they did not play. By the time they began playing in district tournaments, they were quite ready.

One day when the boys were about to begin their practice round,

Mr. Poole came up to the first tee and greeted them. He then called Mario and told him he had something for him. In his hand he held a pair of used golf shoes, which were still in good shape.

"Hello, Mr. Poole," Mario said.

"Mario, I'm sure you can use these on your next shot at state," Mr. Poole proclaimed as he held up the white leather shoes and then handed them to him.

"Gee thanks, Mr. Poole. These are really swell!"

Joe looked at Felipe, smiled, and then whispered that Mario was not too crazy about white shoes, and he bet that Mario would dye them black as he had done before. Felipe nodded in agreement.

It was perfect timing on Mr. Poole's part, as the shoes Mario was wearing that day had already developed holes in the soles. Mario quickly took them off and replaced them with the white ones he had just received.

"They fit perfect, Mr. Poole," Mario said, even though they were a bit big, just like the ones he had gotten from him before. It didn't matter, as he would again stuff them with paper or something else to make the fit more snug. He then tied the old ones together and hung them from his golf bag, as he did not want to throw them away. After they had hit their tee shots on the first hole and had walked up to the green, out of Mr. Poole's sight, Mario took his white shoes off, pulled the small pieces of rag from inside of the old ones, and squeezed them into the new ones. He then placed them back on his feet, stood up, and said, "Now they're really perfect!"

By the time the boys got around to the eighteenth hole, J. B. and Hiram were waiting for them. When they had all putted out on the green, they gathered around J. B.

"Boys, we're going to have a tune-up match before we begin our district play. We will be playing with the Del Rio boys again. They have asked us for a rematch, as I'm sure you remember they were not too happy that you beat them the last time."

"Yeah, we kicked their butts that time!" Mario exclaimed. "Yeah!" the rest shouted in agreement.

"There will also be boys from Eagle Pass and Bandera. This should be a good test for us, as these schools are in Class Double A."

"When is that, Coach?" Felipe asked.

"Next week. After that we will be going to Brownwood to play in the Jaycee Invitational Tournament. Hiram got us in that one after he met their coach last year."

"We're ready for them, Coach!" Joe pronounced. "Yeah, we can kick their butts too!" Gene chimed in.

"I know you can, but I still want you all to practice hard over the next several days," J. B. cautioned.

"Of course, Coach," Mario replied. "We always practice hard!"

J. B. and Hiram laughed but approved of the confidence expressed by the young warriors. Then Hiram warned them, "Ranger will be at Brownwood, so this is a good chance for a rematch against them. If we make it to state again, we're likely to see them there as well."

"You mean, 'when we go to state!'" Mario emphasized.

"You're right, Mario but let's not get ahead of ourselves," J. B. admonished. "We've got to do it one step at a time. I want you guys to spend some time on the practice putting green right now. I know you want to go to your *Llanito* place, but you need some time on real greens."

"Sure, Coach!" Joe acknowledged as the boys gathered their bags and headed for the practice green, where they spent time putting balls for the next hour as the sun went down.

CHAPTER SIXTEEN

THE TOURNAMENT WAS CALLED "Golfest 1957" by its organizer, Joe Hendry, the new head pro at San Felipe Country Club. The teams from Del Rio, Bandera, Eagle Pass, and San Felipe high schools gathered at the club on this Saturday in the early part of the year. The San Fe boys showed no signs of nervousness, as they were intimately familiar with each blade of grass at the course, having not only played there many times, but also having caddied for the members for years. The Del Rio boys were also familiar with the course, as it was their home course. At a disadvantage were the kids from Bandera and Eagle Pass, who might have had one or two members of their teams who had played the course before.

Joe got to play with Joe Ricks from Del Rio High, for whom he had caddied on occasion along with his father, as well as a boy from Bandera and one from Eagle Pass. Felipe was paired with Del Rio player Jay Vineyard, along with those from Eagle Pass and Bandera. In his foursome, Mario Lomas was teamed up against John Pettit from Del Rio and two boys from the other schools. Lupe Felan was matched against Don Ricks from Del Rio together with the two from the visiting schools. Finally, Gene Vasquez began his high school competition days with a match against Hank Moody from Del Rio and the boys from the out-of-town schools.

Without feeling an ounce of pressure, having now become accustomed to playing competitive golf, and having played the course over a hundred times, Joe began the round with an easy kick-in birdie. His round progressed in much the same way it had done many times at San Felipe in the past. He was ahead of Ricks by three strokes going into the last hole, so Joe figured that if he beat him, the team would do well, as he felt Ricks was Del Rio's best player. He approached the eighteenth tee with plenty of confidence in his swing. He set up and stared at his ball on the tee.

"I'm going to hit this ball inside ten feet from the hole!" he thought to himself. He then took his swing, striking the ball almost perfectly, and watched it as it quickly rose into the air in the direction of the flag on the green.

"It's there!" Ricks exclaimed, knowing that Joe had hit another fine shot.

Sure enough. The ball hit on the front edge of the green, bounced once, and then rolled to three feet away from the hole.

"Great shot, Joe!" Ricks shouted as the other players stood silently staring at the shot and then at Joe.

"Thanks, Joe!" Joe replied.

Ricks then hit his shot, and although he managed to get on the green, the ball remained about twenty feet from the stick. The other two players in the group came up short on their shots and would have to chip up to try to save par.

Despite having more bogeys than he had hoped, Joe was happy with his round. A birdie on the last hole would give him a seventy-eight for the day and put him four strokes ahead of Ricks. By the time he reached the green, J. B. and Hiram were waiting for him. Joe smiled at both and then walked over to mark his ball so that the two players who had missed the green could chip up.

"Oh, he's playing well," declared Hiram as he turned to J. B. "I think you're right," J. B. said.

They watched the boys make their final strokes for the day. First, the boys who had missed the green bogeyed the hole. Then, Joe Ricks narrowly missed his long birdie putt and then tapped in for par. Finally, Joe stepped up to his ball and stroked it smoothly into the hole for his birdie. After shaking the hands of his competitors, Joe walked over to where J. B. and Hiram were standing.

"How'd you do, Joe?" J. B. asked. "Seventy-eight!" Joe replied.

"That's good. That's very good, Joe," J. B. commented. "Good going!" Hiram agreed.

"Thanks!" Joe said in his usual humble tone.

"That puts us in the lead," Hiram pointed out to J. B.

"Yes! Let's hope we can hang on to it," J. B. cautiously agreed.

Felipe, in the second group, was also enjoying a good day. A few bogeys and a double bogey had hurt his round, but a couple of birdies and an eagle on the seventeenth hole helped him bring his score on pace to shoot eighty if he could birdie the last hole. This would also put him ahead of his nearest competitor from across the creek. J. B. and Hiram were waiting for him at the last hole, and they could see him getting ready to hit his tee shot.

With the strong, fluid swing produced by his thin arms and frame, Felipe hit his shot onto the green, thus giving himself a chance to birdie the final hole. He was the only one of his group reaching the green with his tee shot. When he arrived on the green to check out his ball, J. B. and Hiram were waiting. Felipe marked his ball, picked it up, and then turned to them and smiled. Again J. B. and Hiram could tell the day was going well for Felipe. Once the other three players finished up, Felipe took his turn to try for a birdie. He struck the ball with confidence, but alas, the ball slipped by the edge and stopped less than a foot away from the hole. He tapped it in for a total score of eighty-one.

J. B. and Hiram greeted him with a pat on the back and then vocally complimented him on the round. Against the eighty-four that Joe Ricks shot and the ninety-three that Jay Vinyard carded, the Mustangs were eighteen shots ahead of the Del Rio squad, who stood at second place. The boys from Eagle Pass and Bandera found themselves even further removed from the leaders.

Next to come in was Mario and his three competitors. Mario was his typical jovial self as he walked toward the last green. That meant that he too was enjoying a good round, while the other three had the look of disappointment in their faces. By the time Mario was able to hole out on the last green, his seventy-nine had outpaced his nearest competitor, John Pettit, by ten strokes. J. B. and Hiram, who were now joined by Joe and Felipe, clapped in approval as Mario pulled the ball out of the hole. The only ones left were Gene and Lupe.

"If Gene and Lupe come in with their typical scores for the round, we'll take this thing!" Hiram said to J. B., who nodded in agreement.

"Yeah, the Del Rio boys would have to make up twenty-eight strokes to beat us, and their best players have already finished," J. B. commented.

Before too long, Gene and his group approached the final hole with the now-bigger crowd of Mustangs waiting. None of the four had hit the green, but only Gene had been able to get up and down for par. After shaking the hands of his playing competitors, Gene walked over to J. B. and the other boys.

"How did it go for you, Gene?" J. B. asked.

With a smile on his face, Gene answered proudly, "Shot an eighty-four, Coach!"

"That's very good, son!" J. B. replied. He knew now that Del Rio would not be able to catch up, since Hank Moody from Gene's group had shot a ninety-two. Unless Lupe shot more than thirty-six shots over his typical round or his competitor from the other side of the tracks shot the same amount of strokes below his, it was over. That was not likely to happen, he thought to himself.

Sure enough, when Lupe's group came in, the coach learned that the Del Rio boy, Don Ricks, had scored better than Lupe but only by four strokes, giving the Del Rio team a total score of 358, making it the runner-up to the Mustangs. The Mustangs' total was 322, a full thirty-six strokes better than their crosstown rivals.

After J. B. and his team accepted congratulations from Joe Hendry, as well as the other coaches, J. B. gathered his team.

"This was a good practice for us, but I'm sure you know that Ranger is going to be tougher than the teams we beat today. We can enjoy this victory, but tomorrow we have to get ready for the Jaycee Invitational in Brownwood."

"Sure thing, Coach! We'll get better!" Mario asserted.

"Yeah! Yeah!" the rest agreed.

"We'll be ready!" Joe added.

"Okay then! I'll see you all here tomorrow after school," J. B. instructed.

The boys weren't going to wait until the next day to practice. Without any of them saying a word, they all headed out with their golf bags on their shoulders en route to their sanctuary, the El Llanito Country Club.

CHAPTER SEVENTEEN

Aᴄᴛᴇʀ ᴅᴏᴍɪɴᴀᴛɪɴɢ ᴛʜᴇ Bʀᴏᴡɴᴡᴏᴏᴅ tournament just as they had done at Golfest, the boys began getting ready for the district tournament. They traveled to Crystal City as the defending champions, but this mattered not to the boys. They wanted to prove worthy of a trip back to state, and the district competition was the first step on their quest.

J. B., as their coach, knew quite well there was minimal danger of the boys becoming too confident. After all, confidence on the golf course was a good thing. It promoted good fluid swings. However, J. B. wanted to make sure the boys maintained their focus solely on the round today.

"Boys, I'm sure all of you want to get back to state, and no doubt we can do that. However, we cannot get ahead of ourselves. The only thing that matters now is the round you will be playing today! Are you with me on this?" J. B. asked emphatically.

"We know, Coach!" Mario asserted. "We're with you!" "That's right, Coach," Joe added.

"Yeah!" Felipe, Gene, and Lupe chimed in.

"All right, then. Let's go out there and play like you know how!" J. B. urged.

The district tournament proved to be not much of a test, as the Mustangs cruised to a twenty-six-stroke victory. They would now be traveling to San Marcos in two weeks for the regional competition in Class A high school golf.

Two weeks later the competition, though better than in district, was unable to foil the Mustangs' plans. Their victory in the regional tournament gave them the pass that they had been waiting to earn for a year.

A week before they were to travel to Austin for the big game, J. B. gathered his troops for some sad announcements.

"Fellas, everyone is pleased with your success and our chance to win the state tournament, knowing that we came close last year," J. B. began. "But I have some not-so good news from the school board." J. B. paused, feeling distressed by what he would say. "I have been told that we can only take four of you to Austin!"

The boys' reaction was quick and predictable. "Why, Coach?" Joe asked.

"And which four?" Felipe jumped in.

"Look. I know all the schools enter five players in the tournament, even though the scores of only the best four are counted. The board said to me that they can only afford to send four players, and those four are going to be our best golfers," J. B. tried to explain.

"Well who's gonna decide which are the best four, Coach?" Mario asked.

J. B. took his time answering, as he did not want any of his players to get hurt and disappointed. "Well, we know that Joe, Mario, and Felipe are the best three of the group, right?" J. B. asked for affirmation.

"I guess!" Joe said softly as he looked to the others for confirmation.

"I suppose you're right, Coach!" Mario affirmed, with Felipe in agreement.

"Okay, so what I was thinking was that on the one hand, I would like to have Lupe play, since he's a senior and all, but I can't ignore the fact that on several occasions, Gene, you have played better in the tournaments we have won. So the only fair thing to do is to have a playoff between Gene and Lupe, and the winner will be our fourth."

"That's fair, Coach," Lupe said.

"Yeah, that's fair," Gene acknowledged.

"Okay. Good. So Lupe, Gene, you boys get ready and we'll have the playoff right now," J. B. instructed.

"Sure!" Lupe replied. "Okay," Gene added.

To avoid putting any more pressure on the two competitors, Hiram suggested that the two play by themselves, with Hiram as the monitor.

The other three players could play their practice rounds in their own group, and J. B. would follow them. J. B. agreed, and they all headed to the first tee.

The three boys who would not need to play for their spots on the team shared the sentiments expressed by J. B. They would like to see Lupe play in his final tournament because he was a senior, and Gene would have other chances, since he was only a freshman. However, they quietly knew that Gene could often play better than Lupe despite being so young. Today they would not cheer for either one but only hoped that the better of the two would show it by his score.

Of the two, Lupe seemed more nervous and showed it on the first tee. He knew the pressure was on him as he accepted that he had to prove to all that he deserved to be on the team, not because he was older and a senior, but because the team needed the better golfer going to the state tournament.

His first shot didn't hit the green on the par-three first hole. Neither did Gene's, but he was able to get up and down for par, while Lupe settled for a bogey. This pattern continued throughout the round. Gene would par a hole, and Lupe would bogey it. Gene would bogey a hole, but Lupe would double bogey it. When Lupe managed to get a par, so did Gene. Lupe never seemed to be able to shake the younger player. In the end, Gene bested Lupe with his eighty to Lupe's eighty-five.

The other boys came over to Gene and quietly shook his hand in congratulations but said little. They walked over to Lupe and patted him on the back. It seemed all were resigned to the fact that Lupe would not be able to join them in Austin. J. B. pulled Lupe aside and privately said something to him, and Lupe nodded affirmatively. J. B. then walked over to Gene and said he wanted to talk to him privately, and Gene acquiesced.

"Son, I know you won fair and square, and you showed a lot of courage out there. Lupe just had a bad day and probably was a little too nervous. Ahh, would you be willing to do a rematch and give Lupe another chance to be on the team? It would mean a lot to me," J. B. pleaded.

Without taking any time to think, Gene responded, "Sure, Coach!"

"Thank you, son!" J. B. said. "You're a big man for doing this!"

"Okay," Gene said matter-of-factly.

"Good, then we'll have the rematch tomorrow after school," J. B. stated.

"That's fine, Coach," Gene agreed.

The next day they all showed up at the club for another practice round and the rematch between Gene and Lupe for the fourth spot on the team. The two began the round under the supervision of Hiram, who privately could not decide whom he would like to see on the team. He just wanted to see that the two played their best and by the rules.

On the first tee, Gene was still thinking that maybe he should just let Lupe take the spot, but he remembered what Joe had told him the night before. The team needed the best four players to compete against the other schools at state, especially Ranger, which had beaten them last year. If Gene could show that he was one of the best four, there was no reason for him to bow out. He deserved to be on the team if he played his best and his best was better than Lupe's. He took a deep breath and set out to play his heart out. He would be happy if he made the team, and he would be happy if Lupe outplayed him. That was the mindset he employed throughout the entire round.

Lupe, on the other hand, felt even more pressure today. He did not want to disappoint the coach, who had convinced Gene to give him another chance, but he clearly understood that he did not want to be on the team if he wasn't able to prove that he deserved the spot. To do so, he would have to beat the young freshman, and he hadn't been able to do that for many of the rounds that they had played together.

Though he was able to play better than the previous day, his score was not low enough to beat Gene's. His eighty-two was closer than yesterday, but Gene's repeat of an eighty sealed his fate, or at least that's what everyone thought.

With visible disappointment on his face, J. B. gathered all the boys before him. Without talking to either Lupe or Gene, J. B. expressed what he was thinking. "That was a close round, and both of you played well. I think you both deserve to be on the team, but with the scores being that close, it's too hard to decide who should go to Austin with us!"

"But Coach, Gene won fair and square and he should go!" Joe pointed out in amazement.

J. B. insisted on pleading his case on behalf of Lupe. "I know, but Lupe is a senior, and he's never again going to get a chance to play in another state tournament." He stopped himself, as he was now appearing to be playing favorites and he did not want to deprive Gene of what was rightfully his. He thought for a moment and then said, "Gene, I don't want to keep you from this team, but would you be willing to give Lupe another chance, please?"

Gene thought quietly and then looked at Joe, Mario, and Felipe, who said nothing. He then looked at Lupe and thought about what he had said to Joe two nights before. He didn't want to give up his place on the team, but if he could beat Lupe one more time, then nobody could tell him that he did not deserve to be on the team. "Sure, Coach!" he said. "I'll do it."

"Thank you, Gene. That's mighty kind of you," J. B. uttered.

Lupe was feeling embarrassed that he had not been able to demonstrate by his skills that he should be on the team. He walked over to Gene and said, "Thanks, Gene. You're the best! If you beat me again, you're going to Austin, no matter what Coach says!"

Gene smiled and shook Lupe's outstretched hand.

The next day the group gathered at the site where Lupe's fate would be determined for good. For some unexplained reason, neither of the boys experienced any pressure. Gene was resigned to accept that his swing alone would show everyone who deserved to go to Austin. Lupe understood that if his game was truly better than Gene's, it would show up on its own without being forced out by anything he did. If it was meant to be that he go to state, then he would prevail over Gene. If not, he would be happy that the best four players would be making the trip.

Despite every effort on his part, Lupe was not able to grant J. B. his wish as Gene once again turned in the better score and secured his spot on the team.

CHAPTER EIGHTEEN

AFTER A YEAR OF waiting for another chance to win the ultimate prize in Texas high school golf competition, the Mustang Golf Team arrived in Austin ready for the rematch against the '56 winners, Ranger High School. Along with Ranger, teams from Shamrock, Liberty, Pine Tree, Martin, and Mercedes high schools had sights on thwarting the Mustangs' quest. The first order of business was to secure a good practice round on the Thursday of their arrival.

As the boys gathered their equipment from his car, J. B. began his instructions. "All right, boys! We need to get acquainted with the course, so let's get out there and pay close attention to your surroundings. Memorize each hole so you know where you need to hit it tomorrow and Saturday."

"Don't forget to play smart and not try something you haven't done before!" added Joe Mitchell, the old pro from San Felipe Country Club, who had developed a good friendship with J. B. and Hiram and had been asked by them to join the group.

All the boys nodded in agreement.

"What time's our tee time, Hiram?" asked J. B.

"We're on the tee in fifteen minutes, Coach," he replied.

"Well, that doesn't give us time to hit the range, but it's just a practice round, so that's not a problem. Boys, just loosen up before you hit the first ball," J. B. instructed.

"We'll do, Coach!" Joe replied, and Felipe, Mario, and Gene nodded in agreement.

The boys then headed for the first tee box and waited for their turn as they watched the team from Ranger tee off. Joe turned to his teammates and said, "There they are, guys! Our main competition!"

"We can kick their butts!" Mario boasted. "Yeah!" Gene added as Felipe smiled.

When the Ranger boys had cleared the fairway, the starter motioned to them that they could now hit away. One by one they sent their balls flying down the fairway. It was a good start, and J. B., Hiram, and Joe Mitchell were pleased as they followed the boys along the course.

The boys seemed to be in sync, as each managed to keep up with the rest, hole after hole. No one encountered any great difficulties with the course, and they seemed to manage each hole like experienced linksters. In the end, Mario turned in the best score at seventy-nine, but Joe and Felipe were only one shot higher at eighty. Gene came in at eighty-one, so J. B. and the others felt confident that the boys were ready for the big show.

After being treated to a great meal by Hiram, the boys settled in for a good night's rest.

The next morning, the group anxiously arrived at the course, this time with plenty of time to hit balls at the practice range. When they were walking up to the range, some of the other players were already hitting balls.

One of them turned to another and, while pointing at the Mustangs, said, "Hey look! It's the beaners. They're back for another beating!" Laughter followed.

The Mustang golfers resisted all temptation to react to what they heard, and no one said a word. In their typical uniforms of T-shirts and jeans, they each set up their bags on the range and began their warm-up under the watchful eye of Joe Mitchell, whose main purpose there was to make sure the boys' swings remained the same as they had been developed by years of practice at San Felipe.

As Joe placed ball after ball by his feet and hit them, he could tell someone else besides Mr. Mitchell was gazing at his swing. The tall, slender man with glasses stood by Joe Mitchell with his arms crossed in front of him and stared at Joe as he took swings with several clubs. Each time the ball sailed straight out in the direction Joe was aiming. After several minutes of watching Joe, the man got closer and commented.

"Son, who taught you that swing?" the stranger asked.

Joe turned to the man and replied, "No one, sir. I saw it in a golf book once."

"Well, don't ever let anyone change it. You've got a very good and sound swing. Just keep it up!"

"Thank you, sir," Joe replied as the man walked away without saying anything more.

Joe Mitchell, who had heard the man's comments to Joe, asked, "Do you know who that is, son?"

Joe shook his head and said, "No, sir. Who was he?"

"That was Harvey Penick! He's the pro here at Austin Country Club and is well known as a golf instructor. If he liked your swing, then you know you've got something, Joe!"

"That's good, huh?" Joe asked surprised. "You'd better believe it!" Mr. Mitchell added.

"Just don't let it get to your head!" Mario admonished jokingly, having heard what was going on.

"Heck no!" Joe replied. "I already knew I had a good swing!"

"Yeah and that Peanut guy just proved it," Mario continued. "That's 'Penick,' Mario. Not Peanut," Mr. Mitchell corrected him.

Joe and Mario laughed and grabbed their bags, having finished their warm-up.

"Let's go putt some," Joe suggested.

"Okay," Mario said, and he began following Joe to the practice green. Felipe and Gene quickly joined them as well.

As Mario placed some golf balls on the green to begin putting, a tall, muscular white boy wearing a Shamrock High School shirt walked up to him. He looked down at Mario's feet and began his quips.

"You know, kid. I have some golf shoes just like those," he said, pointing at Mario's shoes. "Someone stole them from me last night, and I was told it was a Meskin who did it. I bet you have my shoes, boy!"

Mario was caught off guard and couldn't see through what the boy was doing. "They're not your shoes!" he protested. "These are my shoes!"

Despite Mario's protests, the boy continued. "Nah! Those look like my shoes. They're black and look like my size," he insisted.

"They can't be your shoes, and I can prove it!" Mario exclaimed while he sat down on the green. He scratched his right one with a wooden tee he had pulled from his pocket to remove a little of the black polish that he had used to cover the once-white shoes. "See!" Mario pointed out to the boy. "I bet your shoes weren't white first and then painted black like mine, right?"

The boy looked at Mario and shook his head but said nothing as he walked away.

Felipe, who had been standing near Mario in case anything worse than an exchange of words occurred, said, "Mario, don't you know what he was trying to do? He was just trying to mess with your head so you would screw up during the round."

"Yeah, he was just messing with you," Joe added. "Don't let it get to you."

"Well he better not be playing in my group, 'cause I'll kick his butt!" Mario boasted.

"This isn't a boxing match, Mario! It's golf. Keep your head straight!" Joe admonished.

Mario tried to say something else, but all he could do was laugh. The others joined in.

"See, I told you, you shouldn't have painted those shoes black," Joe continued. "You should have kept them just like Mr. Poole gave them to you."

"Well I don't like white," Mario argued. "White's a sissy color."

"C'mon. Let's do some putting," Joe urged.

The boys spent some time getting used to the green, and they felt pretty confident that if the practice green accurately represented the greens on the course, they would have little problem putting well. It was now time for the first group to go out. This included Joe.

"From Dale Reeo San Filipi, Joe Treyveeno!" announced the starter.

Joe walked up to the tee markers, placed his ball on a tee, and calmly gazed at the fairway in front of him. Without wasting much time, he addressed the ball and relying on the swing that had been admired by the legendary Harvey Penick earlier, Joe pounded the ball in the proper direction, right down the gut of the fairway.

The next player up was the boy who had given Mario a hard time about his shoes. Upon seeing him, Joe turned to Mario, who had noticed the coincidence.

Mario silently mouthed to Joe, "Kick his butt for me!"

Joe nodded affirmatively. When the other players in the group had hit their shots, Joe grabbed his bag and began the walk to his ball. The Shamrock player looked at Joe as he walked, but neither said a word. The silence would continue throughout the entire round.

When Joe arrived at his ball, he saw that the lie was perfect. "I'm getting this ball on the green," he thought. Having outdriven his competitors, he waited for them to hit their shots first. The Shamrock boy hit his shot onto the green and then made it a point to look at Joe, but Joe ignored him. Joe then set up for his shot. With the confident swing of an experienced competitor, Joe hit his ball onto the green about five feet closer to the hole than the Shamrock boy's. Joe was tempted to stare back at him but decided to look ahead and walked straight to the green.

After the two players who had missed the green on their approach managed to come onto the green, the Shamrock boy hit his putt. He thought he had made it, but the ball turned away from the hole on the last five inches. He then tapped the ball in from less than a foot away. It was now Joe's turn.

Joe calmly lined up his putt. It would break slightly to the right, he determined. He took a practice stroke as he was over the ball and then struck it smoothly. The ball rolled on the right path and just as he had calculated, the ball turned slightly right and dropped in the hole for a birdie. He did not make a sound, but inside he was yelling, "That's how I wanted to start!"

"Good putt," uttered one of the other players.

"Thanks," Joe mumbled as he pulled the ball from the hole and the other player replaced the flag.

Back on the first tee, it was Mario's turn to begin play.

The starter then announced, "Next from Dale Reeo San Filipi, Mareeo Lowmus."

Hearing the semblance of his name announced, Mario set up and striped his drive down the fairway. It was going to be a good day for him, he thought. "If I can start this hole with a par, I can give my team a chance."

By the time he reached his ball on the fairway, Joe and his group had already vacated the first green. It was clear for him to hit. He saw the flag on the back side of the green and by the markers on the ground; he figured it would take a five-iron to get the ball on the putting surface.

"Okay, now. Solid swing!" he said to himself. He caught the ball a little fat, but it still managed to bounce onto the front part of the green. "That's gonna be a long putt," he thought. "Just get the first one close," he muttered.

Mario had been paying just enough attention to see where the other players were, but he was otherwise oblivious to their game.

One of the other players called out, "Hey, wetback! It's your turn!"

Mario quickly turned to him with a stern look but said nothing. He approached his putt and squatted down to try to see the line from his ball to the hole. He then stood over his ball, took two practice strokes, and then let it ride. The ball rolled along the surface, occasionally bouncing up upon hitting little bumps in the grass, and stopped about a foot short of the hole.

"Can I finish?" he asked politely.

"Yeah, get it outta the way!" answered the one closest to him.

Mario then looked to make sure he would not step on anyone's line and coaxed the ball in the hole.

"Par's good!" he said to himself as he pulled the ball from the hole and got out of the way.

Next to participate in the Mustang's quest for gold was Felipe.

"On the tee, from Dale Reeo San Filipi, Filipi Romayro," the starter announced.

"I guess he's calling me," Felipe thought, so he walked up to the markers and teed up his ball to begin the round. Following an easy practice swing, Felipe commanded his driver to propel the ball down the fairway. It took an unexpected hop to the right upon landing but stayed on the edge of the fairway.

"That'll work," Felipe reassured himself. He then walked off the tee box to let the other players hit. A par was waiting on the first green to greet him. It was another good start for the purple and gold.

J. B., Hiram, and Joe Mitchell were still spectators on the first tee when it was Gene's turn at the tee. J. B. was still wishing silently that Lupe was the one about to be the fourth on the team but managed a smile in Gene's direction.

"I hope the kid can handle the pressure," Joe Mitchell stated. "He'll do just fine," Hiram said.

J. B. searched in his mind for confidence in the freshman but thought that this being the first real competition for Gene, it would be quite a burden to handle.

Gene was not thinking about the pressure. He just wanted to play with the older boys, and this was the chance he had looked forward to since he started caddying with them. For this is why he learned to play right-handed. He had proven to everyone back home that he belonged on this team, and now he was determined to show it to the rest.

"From Dale Reeo San Filipi, Highgeeneeo Vascuayz!"

"Time to go!" Gene thought to himself as he walked up to the tee box.

While setting up his shot, he felt his body tightening up but didn't realize that he was feeling quite nervous. "I can do this!" he said to himself.

The first practice swing didn't resemble his normal swing he thought, so he tried it again. "Better!" Then he placed the head of his club behind the ball and began his swing. It was a little faster than what he was used to, and by the time the clubhead came down at the ball, it barely caught the top part, so the ball shot out low to the ground. It kept bouncing and rolling down the fairway in an effort not to embarrass the one who hit it, but it was obviously not the best display of Gene's talent.

"Oh shit!" J. B. exclaimed with a grimace on his face but then stopped short of any further comments. He did not mean to show any reaction to his player's shot as he had purposely kept quiet while watching the boys play since becoming their coach.

Walking down the fairway, Gene kept his cool and acted as though he had struck a fine shot. It was now going to require three shots to the green, but that was okay with him. "Give yourself a chance to par, but make no worse than bogey," he muttered to himself. Moments later, a bogey on his card marked the beginning of his round.

"You want to walk over to the ninth green, Coach?" Joe Mitchell asked J. B., who was visibly worried.

"That's a good idea, J. B.," Hiram added.

"Yeah, okay," J. B. replied, and all three headed out to see the progress of the team.

While Gene was struggling with the first hole, Joe was about to hit his tee shot on the sixth hole, a par three with an elevated green and sand bunkers on both sides with a distance of about 186 yards. Joe couldn't decide which iron to hit. He felt a six-iron would not be enough, and a five-iron could probably send the ball past the green. After pondering his dilemma for a moment, he decided to hit a five-iron but with a bit less force than normal.

Joe took a deep breath and lined up to his target. "An easy five," he said to himself as he took his swing. At the moment he struck the ball, he knew he had hit it with the face of the club slightly open, and the white sphere headed toward the right edge of the green overlooking one of the bunkers. Joe was thinking that the ball would not get to the green." Get up, ball! Go!" he commanded, but the ball didn't listen; it hit the edge and bounced down into the bunker.

Though disappointed, Joe fought the urge to utter any expletive. He remembered that J. B. had gotten after him for displaying his short temper back at San Felipe by cussing and throwing his clubs. Instead, he calmly returned the club to its place in his bag and thought, "Just get up and down for par. No problem."

He had maintained a one under par score with the help of his birdie on the first hole, but now that was in jeopardy. When he reached the bunker, he breathed a sigh of relief, as the ball was not buried and had a decent lie. "I can hit this on," he said to himself. He took his sand wedge, and when he was clear to hit, he took a mighty swing, causing an explosion of sand, which carried the golf ball up and over the lip of the bunker. The ball landed on the green and rolled to about eight feet past the hole. "Now I got a chance for par," he told himself.

When it was his turn to putt, Joe looked from every angle to get the best read of the green. From one side it looked fairly straight, but from behind the hole it appeared that it might break a bit left. "If I hit it firm, that won't matter," he thought. He decided that's what he would do—hit it straight and firmly so that he would take the break out of it. He set up and confidently took the putter back and then struck the ball with a firm stroke. The ball quickly rolled toward the cup. It seemed like it was headed directly at the hole without any deviation. It went over the front edge and Joe thought he had made it, but it then hit the back edge and the hole spit it out. Joe saw the ball bounce up and land outside the hole, where it stayed.

"I guess I hit it too hard," Joe muttered as he walked over and lightly tapped the ball into the hole.

"That was a good putt," one of the players said. "It should've gone in," said another.

The Shamrock player was amazed that his opponent had almost

saved his par but said nothing. Privately he breathed a sigh of relief, as he was now tied with Joe. His joy was short-lived though. On the next hole Joe made an easy par, but the Shamrock player had to settle for bogey when he was unable to get up and down for par. By the time they reached the ninth green, Joe was at even par, while the Shamrock player was one over.

"How's it going, Joe?" J. B. asked.

"I'm even, Coach," Joe replied.

"You're at even par?" J. B. asked excitedly.

"Yeah, Coach, but I should've been one under."

"That's great, Joe! Keep it up!"

"Wow!" said Hiram. "Joe's really playing well!" "That's a damn good score!" Joe Mitchell added.

Joe smiled and walked briskly to the tenth tee, as he did not want to give time a chance to interfere with his good round.

By his standards, Mario was not having a good round, although compared to his competitors, he was playing well. He had missed some key putts for par on four of the holes and had to settle for bogeys. When he reached the ninth green, J. B., Hiram, and Joe Mitchell were waiting. Smiles ran across their faces when Mario sank a long putt for par.

"How are you doing, Mario?" J. B. asked as he approached them.

"Not as good as I should be, Coach," Mario responded, with disappointment in his voice.

"What you shoot?" J. B. quizzed. "Forty."

"That's a good score, Mario," Hiram commented. "How did the Ranger boy do?" Joe Mitchell asked.

"Not good. I think he's six or seven over. The Shamrock guy is good. He's two over."

"That's surprising," J. B. said. "It looks like Shamrock is the team to worry about."

"Yeah. Both the Ranger boys we've seen go by seem to be having trouble," Joe Mitchell pointed out.

Hiram began his calculations. "The scores of the two Shamrock players are thirty-seven and thirty-eight, for a total of seventy-five," he said. "Our scores are thirty-six and forty, for a total of seventy six. We're one stroke down!"

"Things look okay for us so far then!" J. B. cautiously exclaimed. "Yeah, we're in this thing!" Joe Mitchell added.

"Any idea which are the best players for Shamrock?" J. B. asked.

"Well, most schools send out their best players first, so we've probably seen them go through," Hiram observed.

"Yeah, and we still have Phil coming in," Joe Mitchell commented. "He's our second-best player, right?"

"You're right," J. B. acknowledged. "Hope Felipe is having a good round!"

It wasn't long before Felipe's group approached the ninth green. J. B. and his companions waited anxiously to learn how their player was doing. They didn't see any balls on the green, so they surmised that Felipe had not reached the putting surface on his second shot. They next saw him stop on the left side of the green and look down, indicating that's where his ball had landed. He then pulled out his pitching wedge, and his swing gently sent the ball onto the green, stopping about five feet from the hole. After marking his ball, he made way for the others to hit their shots toward the flag. This is when he finally looked at J. B. and the others and smiled.

"Oh. He's playing well!" J. B. thought.

Shortly after, Felipe's turn at the hole came up. He took a look at his mark from the back side of the hole and then walked around to get behind his mark in the direction of the hole. He squatted down and placed his ball by the mark and picked up the dime and placed in his pocket. He then stepped next to the ball, placed his putter head behind it, and gave it a gentle tap. In less than a second, the ball fell in the hole. He had made his par. After retrieving his ball, he walked over to J. B.

"How's it going, son?" J. B. asked.

"Okay," Felipe answered nonchalantly.

"What you shoot?" Joe Mitchell asked.

"Thirty-nine, sir."

"That's good," Joe Mitchell commented.

"Well, keep it up, Phil!" J. B. said encouragingly.

Felipe nodded and walked quickly to catch up with his playing partners.

Hiram had walked over to where the Shamrock coach was standing and overheard what his player had scored on the front nine. He eagerly returned to where J. B. and Joe Mitchell were situated. "The Shamrock kid shot a thirty-eight!" he reported.

"That means we're just two strokes down!" Joe Mitchell pointed out.

"That doesn't look too bad, does it?" J. B. wondered out loud.

"Heck no!" Hiram replied. "We're still in it!"

"Yeah! We're still right there!" Joe Mitchell added.

Where San Felipe stood was now dependent on Mario, but he was having some difficulties with some of the holes. He had double bogeyed the fifth hole but birdied the sixth. Then he quickly lost the putting touch on the seventh and eighth holes, ending up with two straight bogeys. Going into the ninth, he was three over par, and the pulled drive off the ninth tee meant he could not reach the green in two. All he could do was punch out onto the fairway and try to hit the dance floor on three.

Mario saw that the coach and his "assistants" were standing by the green when he went to address his ball. "I gotta get this ball on the green now!" he nervously told himself. In response to his swing, the ball flew up in the direction of the flag, but when it descended onto the green, it could not stop rolling. It ended up about twenty feet past the pin.

J. B. grimaced as he saw the ball roll by the flag, and he looked at the others.

"Ohh, he can make that!" Joe Mitchell insisted.

J. B. just shook his head but said nothing. Hiram shook his head in agreement with Joe.

The group made its way onto the green under the watchful eye of all the coaches, who were each anxious to see how their players were doing.

As Mario looked at his ball and then the flag marking the hole, he was visibly disappointed but clearly focused on the task at hand. He had to make the putt if he wanted to break forty on the front nine. Being the farthest one from the hole, he was the first to attempt to sink the putt. He studied the line carefully and then set up for the par-saving stroke. He took several practice strokes as he thought, "I gotta get this putt close to the hole so if I miss, I'll have an easy one for bogey!"

With a healthy stroke at the ball, he sent it on its path toward the hole. He quickly realized that it would not go in, as he missed the line by about an inch to the left. "Maybe it'll break right near the hole," he thought. It did not. However, it stopped a foot past the hole, leaving him a short, easy putt, which gave him a score of forty for the first nine holes.

The Ranger boy was next to putt, and he missed a six-footer for bogey and ended up with a score of forty-three. The Shamrock boy had a five footer for birdie but also missed it. But he shot a thirty-eight for his nine-hole score.

"You're doing just fine, son!" Joe Mitchell complimented Mario when he walked close to him.

"Yeah! You're in good shape, Mario!" Hiram agreed.

"Hang in there!" coaxed J. B. as he wrote down the scores of the golfers. "We're now four strokes down," he said nervously. "It's now going to rest on how Gene is doing."

"That's okay," Joe offered. "The kids from Shamrock and Ranger are also freshmen, so little Gene can hang with them."

"Let's hope so," J. B. commented. He had reservations.

"Well, we'll know pretty soon," Hiram said as he saw Gene and his group halfway down the fairway.

They saw Gene hit a shot toward the green, but it did not make it on. They could not tell if this was his second shot or not, but obviously the young lad was having some problems. None of the other boys hit the green either, and it looked like they had taken more than three swipes to get close.

"Maybe Joe's right!" J. B. thought. "If Gene can stay close to the other players, then we might have a chance!"

By the time Gene hit his ball onto the green, Hiram was trying to get his attention. Hiram jerked his head upward and stretched open his hands at the same time to silently ask Gene how he was doing. Gene saw him and stared out back toward the fairway, poking at the air with his finger to count in his mind the number of shots he had already hit. He then held up five fingers and pointed down toward his ball. He was laying five with a putt coming up for six was the message.

The spectators on the ninth green saw three players besides Gene take at least two putts to hole their balls. They had to have shot six or worse, J. B., Hiram, and Joe Mitchell assumed. It was now Gene's turn. With the fearless confidence that youth sometimes brings, Gene hit the ball without making any practice swings and—"bloop"—the ball went in for a double-bogey six. He picked up his ball and walked over to his supporters.

"How's it going, Gene?" J. B. asked.

"Okay, Coach. Forty-six," Gene replied. This may have seemed a high score, but to Gene it was not too far from where he was used to shooting, and he looked pleased. "The others, not so good."

"What did they shoot?" asked Joe Mitchell.

"I think the Shamrock kid had a forty-two and the Ranger guy a fifty." Gene then shook his head and waggled his hand in disbelief and said, "but the boy from Mercedes had a sixty!"

"Just do your best to keep up, son," J. B. coaxed.

"Sure, Coach. I can do better!" Gene shot back as he moved on to the tenth hole.

"I bet you he can, J. B.," Joe Mitchell challenged.

"Looks like Shamrock is the team we're gonna have to beat," Hiram observed.

"Yep. You're right," J. B. agreed. "We're now eight strokes down to Shamrock."

"Why don't we walk over to the eighteenth green and catch the finish?" Joe suggested.

"All right. Let's see if we can make a move," J. B. replied as the three began their trip to the finish line.

Along the way young Joe was maintaining his steady play. No matter how well the Shamrock boy hit his shots, Joe managed to upstage him. They both parred the tenth, eleventh, twelfth, and thirteenth holes. Joe bogeyed the fourteenth, but the Shamrock player couldn't take advantage of it, bogeying himself. A birdie on the fifteenth by the Shamrock kid was matched by a birdie by Joe. Then they both hit a bump on the way to the sixteenth. Joe's drive off the tee got him in trouble, forcing him to lay up before the water pond fronting the green and try to salvage par with his short iron play and putter. The Shamrock boy, seeing Joe in trouble, decided to go for the green from a bad lie on some hard pan.

"That's not very smart," Joe thought to himself, as he knew the shot required a special touch to pull off. Sure enough, the boy hit the ground about a quarter inch behind the ball, causing the clubhead to bounce up and strike the ball on the upper hemisphere.

"Just as I figured. He topped it," Joe observed silently as he saw the ball bounce, roll close to the ground, and disappear into the pond.

"Fuck!" the boy yelled out, slamming the ground with his club.

Joe then addressed his ball, which was sitting on nice grass in the fairway, and took his swing. The ball sailed high and straight, landing softly on the green about ten feet from the hole. The Shamrock boy wasted no time and dropped his ball in front of the water and took a swipe at it. The ball shot out low but hit the front of the elevated green, bounced up, and landed almost twenty-five feet from the flag. It took him two strokes to sink it, and he walked away with a double bogey. Feeling no pressure, Joe calmly stepped up and hit his putt. It stopped about an inch from the hole, but no matter. He had picked up another stroke against his nearest competitor.

Joe was now sitting at one over, but the Shamrock boy was three over with two holes to go. A par on the seventeenth by both players maintained that separation. The other two players in the group had long realized that they were not going to keep up with these two, so they tried very hard to play quietly and stay out of their way.

When they reached the eighteenth tee box, Joe could see the red-faced Shamrock kid wanting to try harder. He was taking some strong practice swings, making it obvious he was going to swing hard to get his ball in position to go for the green in two on this par-five hole. Joe forced himself not to do the same. He walked up slowly and calmly to the tee and took his normal practice swing. "Smooth as silk," he thought to himself and that's what he did, a perfect drive down the middle of the fairway about 255 yards out.

"Good shot!" one of the other boys said, much to the dismay of the Shamrock player.

The Shamrock boy then set up to the box. As with his practice swing, he took a mighty cut at the ball. He caught it flush, and it too sailed down the middle of the fairway about twenty yards past Joe's.

"Wow! What a shot!" the same kid shouted in amazement, but the Shamrock boy failed to acknowledge the compliment. Once the other two hit their shots, the four walked briskly toward their balls.

From where Joe's ball was situated, the hole had a slight dogleg right with some trees bounding that side of the fairway. "This is gonna take a little cut shot," Joe strategized in his mind. "Probably with my four-wood." There was no real trouble around the green except for a lone bunker to the left, but he knew he would not be reaching it, so that's the shot he planned. He took out the four-wood from his bag and set up to hit his shot. With the same swing that had brought him to this point, he sent the ball flying into the sky, fading ever so slightly along the path of the fairway. It landed about 30 yards short of the green, just like he had planned it.

It was now up to the Shamrock boy to try to execute his attack of the flag. He was about 250 yards out, so he practiced some hard swings with his three-wood and then let it rip. The ball flew rather low but straight at the green, as he did not have to contend with the dogleg of the fairway, since he had hit the ball past the bend. The ball hit the front edge of the green and bounced onto the putting surface. However, the hole had been cut on the front portion, and the ball could not stop until it rolled to the end of the green, about thirty-five feet from the hole. Clapping was suddenly heard from the people waiting near the green, including J. B., Hiram, and Joe Mitchell.

"Damn, that was long!" Joe Mitchell said.

"Yeah, but that's three-putt range," Hiram rationalized.

"Where's Joe's ball?" J. B. asked.

"It's about 30 yards short of the flag," Joe responded. "I think that was the smart play for Joe. Lay up and hit a short iron high and soft to get close to the front pin."

That's exactly what young Joe was thinking. He hit an easy sand wedge, and the ball landed about eight feet from the hole. It would now be a putting duel between him and the Shamrock boy. Being away, the Shamrock kid studied his long putt from every angle possible. It seemed for a while that he didn't want to hit the putt, as he took forever to decide how to stroke it. Finally, he figured there would be about a three-foot break from right to left, so he gave it a go. The ball responded well to the stroke, and it looked favorable as it got closer to the hole.

"I think he made it!" Joe thought to himself while maintaining a cool demeanor studying his putt.

It did not. The ball disappointingly kissed the right edge of the hole and rolled along left, stopping about two feet away.

"Shit!" exclaimed the Shamrock boy but amid the "ahhs" of the crowd, few heard him. He walked over to the ball, and without thinking, assuming that a quick straight tap would send it into the hole, he slapped at it. It hit the hole all right but bounced out and stayed on the edge. In shock and disbelief the boy froze for a moment while the crowd "wowed" in unison. He then made sure that his next strike caused the ball to go in. By the time he reached for his ball, his eyes were swelling up with anger and bitter disappointment. Joe could see that the boy was fighting back the tears, having suffered such obvious embarrassment in front of his coach.

"Let's not do that," Joe said, issuing a quiet self-directive. "Let's try to make it but not get stupid."

He aligned his putter behind the ball and made his stroke. It was a good putt, but alas, it was not good enough, as it slid by the hole, stopping less than a foot away. It was a par nevertheless for Joe, which matched that of the Shamrock player. The final count was Joe seventy-three and a seventy-six for his closest competitor. Joe waited on the green with his hand extended, ready to shake the other players' hands as he had been instructed by his coach, but the others ignored him and walked away. Joe turned to where J. B. was, and he could tell that his coach had just witnessed the gesture. J. B. motioned to him to come over to where he and the other men were standing.

"Looks like you played well, Joe!" Joe Mitchell said as he greeted him.

"Yessir, but I wanted that birdie on the last hole," Joe asserted.

"So that would have put you at what, Joe?" Hiram asked.

"A seventy-two. Even par," Joe uttered with disappointment.

"A seventy-three is great, Joe!" J. B. said excitedly. "Way to go!"

"Nice playing there, son!" Joe Mitchell added.

"Thank you, sir!"

"Okay then, so right now we're three strokes ahead of Shamrock, right?" J. B. asked.

"That's right!" responded Hiram.

"Yeah. We made up two on the total we had going into the back nine," Joe Mitchell confirmed.

"Maybe we'll get even closer when Mario and Felipe come in," suggested Hiram.

"We'll see," J. B. said guardedly.

Soon after, Mario's group approached the 150-yard markers of the eighteenth fairway. None of the boys had tried to reach the par five in two. J. B. and the others then saw Mario get ready to hit his approach. They caught his swing and then picked up the ball as it was in the air flying toward the green. They heard the thump made by the golf ball as it hit the green and rolled to about twenty feet past the hole. They had yet to see anybody stick his shot below the hole, with its tricky front pin placement. Mario seemed calm and walked with a little spring in his step. That was a good sign. He didn't even seem bothered when he missed his birdie try and tapped in for par. He too was ignored by competitors when he tried to shake their hands, so he walked over to J. B. and the rest.

"Got another forty," he said before anyone could ask how his day went.

"Well, you're consistent," Joe Mitchell said jokingly. "An eighty's good, Mario," Hiram remarked.

"I guess," Mario stated with resignation in his voice. "How'd Joe do?" he quickly asked.

"He shot a seventy-three!" J. B. replied.

"And the Shamrock guy?" Mario asked.

"A seventy-six!" J. B. said.

"All right!" Mario exclaimed. "He kicked his butt for me!"

Just then Joe returned from a trip to the bathroom. He saw that Mario had finished, so he went up to him, but before he could ask Mario how he did, Mario blurted out, "Thanks for kicking his butt for me, Joe!"

Joe started to laugh and said, "You're welcome. You owe me now!" "Here!" Mario said as he tossed his golf ball to Joe and laughed.

"What did the Shamrock boy who played with you shoot, Mario?" J. B. asked.

"It seems like he shot a seventy-eight, maybe," he answered but was unsure. He redid the math in his head and said, "Yeah. It was a seventy-eight."

"Okay, so now we're just one stroke up on Shamrock," J. B. concluded. "That's what it looks like to me," Joe Mitchell acknowledged.

"Well, let's see how Felipe did," J. B. wondered out loud.

After waiting for an inordinately long while, J. B. and the others finally saw signs of Felipe's group.

"These fellas really got behind," Joe Mitchell observed. "Someone must have had some trouble."

Joe Mitchell was correct in his assumption. The group had spent a little too much time on the sixteenth and seventeenth holes looking for errantly hit lost balls. Fortunately, none was hit by Felipe, but when one player gets behind, they all get stuck with him. He had stayed on the same pace he had experienced on the front nine, except for one extra hiccup, a bogey on the fourteenth. When the group finally reached the green, Felipe did not seem panicked. He signaled three fingers to J. B. and pointed to his ball.

"He's on in regulation," Joe Mitchell pointed out. "He's got a putt for birdie."

"It looks pretty makeable," Hiram noted. "What do you think, about twelve feet, Joe?"

"Yeah. That's what it looks like," Joe Mitchell answered.

By now J. B. was getting a bit nervous, not knowing exactly where Felipe stood in relation to the Shamrock and Ranger players.

"Let's hope he makes it," J. B. wished out loud.

Just then Felipe struck his putt, but he started walking toward it early, as he could tell it had no chance of going in. It got closer to the hole than he had thought, but it left him with a tap-in putt for par. He retrieved his ball, shook one of the other player's hand who chose not to ignore him as the other two had, and then walked over to his coach.

"How was your round, Phil?" J. B. asked.

"I coulda used that birdie on the last hole, Coach," Felipe said. "Woulda given me another thirty-nine!"

"Hey, a seventy-nine is quite good!" Joe Mitchell said encouragingly.

"Thank you, sir!" Felipe replied. "How did Joe do?"

"Seventy-three!" J. B. answered proudly.

"Wow! That's a great score!" Felipe then asked, "So where do we stand, Coach?"

"I don't know. What did the Shamrock kid shoot?" J. B. asked.

"Oh! A seventy-seven, Coach," Felipe answered.

"Oh. Then we're now one stroke down to Shamrock," J. B. observed nervously.

"We shouldn't worry, Coach. I think they've hit us with their best shot," Hiram stated confidently. "I was talking to one of the coaches, who told me that Shamrock whipped everybody they played against this season by an average of twenty-five strokes."

J. B.'s interest was piqued. "Oh yeah?"

"Sure!" Hiram continued. "I don't think we've played our best, and we're keeping up with them. If we're within ten strokes of them in the end, we have a chance!"

"I agree, J. B.," Joe Mitchell jumped in.

"You got a point there, Hiram." J. B. began to see things differently. "It's up to Gene now."

By this time the group that included Gene approached the eighteenth green. The crowd had now increased, as most of the players had already finished and were anxious to see where each team stood.

Joe, Felipe, Mario, and the adults watched as Gene hit his shot onto the green. Gene noticed his teammates, so he held up four fingers and pointed to the ball.

"He's there in four, Coach," Mario interpreted.

J. B. acknowledged that as he turned and looked at Hiram and Joe Mitchell.

"A two-putt bogey won't be bad," Joe Mitchell affirmed.

Sure enough, two putts got the ball in the hole for Gene. Now J. B. and the others waited anxiously to see what his total score was for the round.

Gene walked over and had a big smile on his face. "I did better, Coach!" he said. "A forty-four on the back!"

"That's a ninety!" Hiram pointed out, but J. B. did not seem pleased. "What'd the others shoot?" J. B. asked.

"The Ranger boy shot a ninety-two, and the Shamrock guy an eighty- two," Gene offered.

"Hmm," was all that J. B. said as he wrote the scores down on his tablet and figured out the total for the two top teams, his and Shamrock's. "Looks like we're down to Shamrock by eight strokes," he announced to his team.

The Mustang boys looked at each other and tried to determine if that was bad or really bad.

Hiram stepped in and said, "That's good! Remember what I told you," he reminded J. B. "Under ten strokes, and we got a shot!"

"You're right, Hiram. That was a very good day for us, boys! You did really good!" J. B. stated.

"Don't you mean 'well,' Coach," Felipe corrected him.

J. B. laughed and said, "I stand corrected."

The boys also began to laugh and even more so when Mario said to Felipe, "Ohh, so you're the teacher now."

Felipe gave a humble nod as they all began to walk over to the official scoreboard.

The figures on the board were posted by the tournament officials, and they confirmed what J. B. had calculated with the help of the boys, Hiram, and Joe Mitchell. It was a good day. Not great, but a good day.

CHAPTER NINETEEN

WHILE THE FIRST DAY of the tournament had been partly sunny and dry, the second day started very cloudy with a light rain. J. B. looked out from the window of his motel room and saw that the rain could possibly present a problem for his golfers.

"It's raining out there, Hiram!" J. B. said to his roommate.

"How hard?" Hiram asked.

"It looks light right now, but who knows if it will stay like this or get heavier."

"What happens if it continues to rain and we can't play?"

"Well, if it becomes unplayable, they can either postpone the second round until tomorrow or ...," J. B. paused for a moment, "hell, they can call it after the first round!"

"But that means we lose!" Hiram exclaimed.

"Yes. That would not be fair at all. Let me call the course and see if I can reach a TIL official and see where we stand."

"That's a good idea," Hiram concurred.

J. B. used the phone in the room and was able to reach one of the tournament officials. He listened intently as the official talked. When he hung up, Hiram quickly wanted to know what was said.

"The course got some rain last night, but the greens superintendent says it's playable," J. B. explained. "They'll only call it if there is thunder or lightning."

"Well, we don't have any of that right now," Hiram observed.

"No, but the forecast I heard on the radio doesn't look good," J. B. stated. "We better get the boys and go."

Just then there was a knock on the door. Hiram opened the door and saw Mario standing there.

"Are we gonna get to play today?" Mario wondered.

"Yes! Get everybody ready to go!" J. B. instructed.

"Okay!" Mario replied and ran back to the boys' room.

Within a minute the whole team was waiting by the coach's room and ready to go. They seemed anxious to get going with the second and determinative round.

Although the boys had experienced difficulty going to sleep, they showed much energy. Joe and Mario had spent the better part of the night encouraging each other and trying to instill confidence in all. Joe had emphasized that each had to be as relaxed as possible and not worry about what the other players were doing. "Just play and have fun," Mario said. They spent most of the night relating the crazy adventures the other players had with their wild shots. They took turns describing, in an exaggerated manner, some of the swings they had witnessed during the first day of competition.

It was not only wet outside, the temperature had dropped considerably. It would be a totally different type of game today, but fortunately, it was the same type of weather they had seen in the days of practice preceding the tournament.

On the way to the course, J. B. tried to give some instructions to his players. "Boys, you need to stay within yourselves today. By that I mean don't try to make shots you're not accustomed to, because of the wet conditions. Do you guys understand?"

"We get it, Coach," Joe responded. "I've already set them straight. They'll be ready."

"Yeah, and what about you?" Gene challenged.

"Don't worry about me. I can handle this weather," Joe bragged.

"All right. When we get there, be sure you get used to swinging with extra clothes on. You'll need to make some adjustments," J. B. instructed.

"Okay," they all responded in unison.

They arrived at the course shortly thereafter and, without any instructions necessary, the boys gathered their equipment. That their bags were made from canvas and not leather as those of the other teams meant that they would soak more of the rain and be heavier to carry. The older and worn out grips on their clubs were going to be slicker due to the wetness. Yet, this didn't matter to the boys. Worrying about their implements was not a priority to the young Mustangs. It couldn't be. To them their tools were the best that money could buy because they made them work.

"It's cold!" Gene complained.

"Don't worry about it," Felipe advised. "Just imagine it's a sunny day and think only of your shot."

"Yeah. Take it one swing at a time," Mario added.

"Remember. It's raining for everyone else, so don't even think about it," Joe wisely instructed.

The boys slowly worked their way to the practice range and began their warm-up. While the other players struggled with wet gloves, the Mustangs did not share in that problem, as they didn't use them. They had gotten used to swinging with their bare hands. The calluses they had developed in their hands from hitting so many balls provided all the gripping strength they needed.

Once they had finished with their warm-up, the boys listened as J. B. explained the order of play. They would be going out in the same order as the day before with the same competitors. That suited them just fine. J. B. chose not to tell the boys that if the rain got heavier and the course became unplayable, the officials could call the tournament as final with only one round completed. He did not want to add any unnecessary pressure. He did not want them to try making shots they hadn't perfected before and risk big numbers on the holes. If they played just like in the practice rounds back home, where it had rained in the days leading up to the state contest, they would be okay, he thought.

Having received good wishes from his teammates, Joe headed to the tee box of the first hole. The other three players soon arrived behind him. As Joe had shot the low round the day before, the starter announced that he had the honors and could hit first.

"It's not raining. It's not raining," he thought to himself as he took his opening swing. The blast sent the ball down the middle amid the light drops of moisture. When it landed, it hydroplaned along the wet grass of the fairway, but it was in the right spot for his next shot.

Next was the Shamrock boy, but before he hit his shot, he kept struggling with the grip of his club. He finally realized that his glove was too wet to help, so he took it off in frustration. His decision to go glove-less, although right, meant he would be hitting the club with his bare hands, which was something he was not accustomed to doing. When he failed to slow down his swing to compensate for the less effective grip, the club slipped slightly in his hands, and he thinned the shot. The ball shot out low and somewhat to the right. The unpleasant conditions and his feeble attempts to adjust to them were already determining his state of mind for the rest of the round.

Once the other two players had hit their balls off the tee, Joe grabbed his bag and walked swiftly toward his ball. The quick pace would warm up his body, he felt. He stopped about 30 yards shy of his ball, as the Shamrock player was behind and to the right of Joe's ball and would be hitting first. When Joe heard the "slop" sound coming from the club striking the ground, he knew the Shamrock boy had just hit it "fat." The expletives that followed confirmed it.

Joe forced himself to ignore what he had just witnessed and focused solely on his ball and the plans he had developed in his mind to send it flying to the green. A deep breath preceded his well-grooved swing, and instantly his plan was carried out. His state of mind stood in glaring contrast to that of the Shamrock kid.

The second group then proceeded to the first tee box, and Mario whispered to himself over and over, "Fairways and greens, swing easy. Fairways and greens, swing easy."

"Did you say something?" one of the other players asked him.

"Oh, no!" Mario replied upon realizing that someone had heard him. "Just talking to myself."

When it was his turn to hit, Mario gazed down the fairway and initially saw the green of the grass and thought that's where he was going to send his ball. But then the image of their hole in El Llanito flashed across his view, and he thought, "Just like back home, Mario! Just like back home!"

He was now ready to hit it, and after his one graceful swipe, the ball took off in perfect fidelity with the instructions Mario had given it, flying long and straight, directly down the center of the playing area.

"Good shot!" one of the boys exclaimed before another slapped the boy on his arm, shook his head, and quietly told him that he was not to compliment the wetback.

"Thanks!" Mario said as he picked up his tee and placed the driver back in its bag. He ignored the other boy's comment.

After continuously wiping his hand on his pants, the Shamrock player hit his shot. While it managed to find the fairway, it was not as impressive as Mario's. It started out to the left but then quickly turned to the right. "Damn! I sliced it," the boy said.

When Mario's group moved on closer to the green, the starter called out the players in Felipe's foursome. Felipe waited patiently for the Shamrock player to play away and thought about the first time he had taken a club to a golf ball. It seemed like a long time ago. "I can play this game!" he thought. "We've played in the hot sun, in the cold, and when it's raining. This is nothing!" Indeed, he had every reason to feel confident as these thoughts ran through his mind. It was time to play.

Upon hearing his name announced by the starter, he took the long metal stick with the wooden head and set it down behind his teed-up ball. The calluses on his hands developed by years of smacking balls without gloves provided the much-needed grip on the club. "Thwak" was the loud sound the ball made as it was smashed by the face of the driver. "That was on the screws," he silently observed, and the flight of the ball confirmed it.

To pass the time as he waited for his turn at the tee, Gene was twirling the four-wood in his left hand nervously. He closely inspected each spot of the club, beginning with the head and then the grip. He noticed that the section of the rubber grip that he customarily grabbed, close to the bottom end, was worn down, almost exposing the metal shaft. He gripped it there because the club was too long for him. He had tried gripping it closer to the end, but he kept missing the ball, so he adjusted to it by gripping down closer to the exposed shaft. He gripped the club on the worn area and took a swing. "It still works!" he thought. It was his trusted weapon, and he relied upon it off the tee. Joe, Mario, and Felipe had forbidden him to use the driver because he would always hit a wicked slice, whereas the four-wood would always go straight. In fact, before the round began, Joe had pulled the driver out of Gene's bag and left it in the trunk of J. B.'s car.

One of the other players noticed the condition of Gene's club.

"You can hit the ball with that thing?" he asked while pointing at Gene's four-wood.

"I did yesterday! Didn't you see me?" Gene retorted. The boy said nothing more.

Gene remembered what Joe had told him about playing in the rain. He was determined to follow his advice. When he approached the tee box, he told himself, "Don't worry about anything today except where you want the ball to go." With that he took a swing at his ball using his choked-down grip on the club and sent the ball low but on a good path to the right side of the fairway.

J. B., Hiram, and Joe Mitchell were pleased with the start of their boys' play. "Let's hope we get to finish this round," Hiram wished out loud.

"Yeah! Let's pray it doesn't rain any harder," Joe Mitchell added.

The men repeated their ritual as observers of the team, walking to the ninth green to learn how the boys were doing.

Joe's group had already reached the fifth fairway, where Joe stood waiting once again for the Shamrock kid to get his ball back into play following his errant tee shot. Joe could sense that the kid was starting to give up. The harder he tried to hit his ball correctly, the worse the result. Joe had parred the first three holes but bogeyed the fourth. The Shamrock player had dug himself into a desperate hole even this early in the round. At six over par, he could see himself letting the lead his team had established the day before slip away.

Joe stood over his ball as he confirmed the yardage he had calculated to the flag and prepared for the shot. The rain had indeed gotten more intense, and Joe could feel and see the drops slide down his face and toward the ground. "It's still okay," he thought as he let his swing take over. Much to the Shamrock boy's dismay, the ball flew onto the green, while he still had to use one more stroke to accomplish the same thing.

Once they reached the green, Joe saw that his ball had come to rest about thirteen feet from the hole, but a puddle of water had collected between his ball and the hole. He would have to hit it a bit harder to get it to the hole, he thought. But how much harder? He remembered that on the previous greens the water had resisted the traction of his ball, so the putts had come up short. "Trust your stroke," he commanded himself.

The strike with his putter sent the ball on its way. When it passed through the puddle, Joe could see the cocktail of water following the ball. It had enough momentum to get to the hole, but it missed it by an inch to the left, stopping a foot and a half on the other side. "Okay. I can make this!" Joe assured himself. He did.

The Shamrock boy then hit his putt, and it too missed as he shook his head in frustration. "One more stroke down to the kid from San Filipi," he told himself.

Mario, who was standing on the fifth fairway, saw Joe two-putt. "Okay. He made his par," Mario said to himself. "You can do the same!" By the now the rain and cold had given him the sniffles. He could feel the moisture outside and inside his nose. He wiped his nose with the sleeve of his sweatshirt right before he hit his shot. "Get there!" he commanded his ball. It didn't listen; it fell short and to the left of the green. "That's all right. I can get it up and down," he told himself.

Though he gave it a good try, he was unable to do so. That didn't matter much, as the Shamrock boy struggled to make a seven on the hole after chipping it twice and three-putting. Mario was now two over par for his round, whereas his main opponent was five over.

Felipe's round was going as well as Mario's at this point. A bogey on the second hole followed a par on the first and preceded another par on the third and fourth holes. However, on the fifth, he didn't hit his putt hard enough to get through the same puddle that Joe had encountered on his line, and Felipe bogeyed again. His competitor had not made a single par yet, and the double bogey on three and now five placed him at seven over. The other two in the group were way out of it, as they had not been able to keep their scores under triple bogey on each hole and were now obviously not factors in the competition.

When Gene came around to the fifth green, he seemed to be in control of the group. Though the other players were at the same skill level when the round started, by now he was the only one not seriously affected by the elements. His rounds rarely included birdies or a great number of pars, so there was no sense in setting that as his goal today. No, today his goal was to try to make pars, but if he fell short, to not make any worse than bogey. So far, his plan was working, as he had managed to keep his score at four over par. On the fifth green he had another chance to make a par, but his putt saw the same fate as Felipe's because of the puddle of water. Five over par after five holes of play satisfied his coach and the two friendly spectators.

The ninth green was now entertaining the company of Joe's ball. If he could make the birdie putt, it would erase one of the strokes that hovered over par. The rain had been unrelenting, and Joe fought hard not to be annoyed with the wetness. He told himself he had to follow his own instructions he had given his teammates to ignore the rain. He calmly placed himself parallel to his ball and envisioned the line that he needed to send the ball on. He moved the putter head back and then pressed it forward against the ball. It rolled on the designated line but did not go far enough to get to the hole. A disappointing but acceptable par ended his front nine. The Shamrock boy was not as fortunate, as his putt was for bogey, and he too missed it short. Eight over par marked his halfway point.

After collecting Joe's score at the turn, J. B. smiled at Hiram. "It puts us just two strokes down, guys!" he said excitedly. "We're getting there!"

"I think Muhreeo can put us ahead," Joe Mitchell said.

"If he's playing like he can, we're gonna see a lead change," Hiram hoped out loud.

Mario came to the ninth green all wet, but you wouldn't have known it by his demeanor. He acted as though he were playing back at San Felipe Country Club on a sunny day. He had given himself a chance at a birdie, having hit his approach shot to fifteen feet from the green, which today had the flag farther back. The Shamrock boy was still struggling to get his ball on the green, despite six attempts. The boy hit his chip shot from the opposite side of the hole, and when it hit the green, it rolled straight toward the pin. Upon arrival at the hole, it hit the flagstick and disappeared into the hole. The people who were watching clapped in approval, but the boy just raised his hand in appreciation of the gesture. He could not get excited, as the shot was for double bogey.

Mario thought to himself, "Well it's better than a triple." He then proceeded to line up his putt by crouching down behind the ball in the direction of the hole. He nodded his head up and down, as if he was acknowledging his own confirmation of the right line. The putt he next made was good, but it stopped one inch before the edge of the hole. "How did that stop?" he wondered.

"He parred the hole," Joe Mitchell observed in a whisper to J. B. and Hiram.

"That has to be a good sign!" Hiram said.

It was, as Mario reported a score of three over par for the first nine holes. J. B. happily wrote down a thirty-nine on his tally sheet along with the score of the Shamrock player.

It was now Felipe's turn to arrive at the ninth hole, and J. B., Hiram, and Joe Mitchell were anxiously waiting to learn how he was doing. Felipe joined Joe and Mario on the green in regulation, and he too was looking at a birdie attempt. First, he waited patiently for the other players to get onto the putting surface. The men were looking closely at the Shamrock player and noticed the frown on his face.

"Must not be going well for him," Joe Mitchell observed quietly.

Hiram nodded his head in agreement as the boy tried to sink his putt. The men on the sidelines did not yet know how many strokes he took to end the ninth hole.

Felipe stood over the hole and then walked back to his ball. "I see this line," he said to himself. "Now hit it!" As he gently struck the ball, it stayed true to the line he had picked. Two seconds later it dropped into the hole. The crowd applauded one of the rare birdies of the day. "Yes!" Felipe exclaimed as he slapped his left hand with his right.

"Same as yesterday, Coach!" Felipe reported when he walked over to

J. B.

"What?" J. B. asked. He thought he knew what Felipe meant but wanted confirmation.

"A thirty-nine?" Hiram asked.

"Yessir!" Felipe replied with a smile on his face.

"That is a hell of a score in these conditions!" Joe Mitchell said.

"Thank you, Mr. Mitchell," Felipe humbly responded as he walked toward the next tee.

The three adults turned to each other, but none of them dared say what they were thinking. They had to wait to see what Gene was doing and how he would finish the front.

Before long the group with Gene at the helm reached the green. Gene's demeanor had not changed noticeably, so this increased the anxiety in his coach's mind. J. B. wanted to interpret it as a positive sign, but he reserved his conclusion until Gene finished. He saw Gene take two putts, but it was not clear how that compared to the Shamrock player, who had taken four putts to complete his front nine. Once everyone completed the hole, Gene came over to meet up with J. B. and the rest.

"So what was that for, son?" Joe Mitchell asked, beating J. B. to the question.

"Forty-three, sir!" Gene reported.

"That is just fine, Gene!" Hiram told him.

"Keep it up!" "Stay in there, Gene!" J. B. nervously instructed.

"Of course, Coach!" Gene confidently replied. "I got this!"

J. B., who now seemed to be bothered more by the rain running down his face, wanted to steer clear of the thoughts going through his head. He did not want to get ahead of himself, but it now looked like his boys had a chance to pull it off.

Hiram and Joe Mitchell noticed the look on J. B.'s face and decided it would be best not to say anything for fear of jinxing the boys.

"Let's catch them on eighteen," Hiram suggested, and the three began walking in that direction.

Joe had now reached the seventeenth tee box. The hole had given him some problems before, so he stared at the flag in the distance and told himself, "Today I gotcha!" He then aligned his body in the direction of the hole and let his swing confirm his confident assertion. The ball listened—it hit the middle of the green and stopped ten feet from the hole.

On the par-three seventeenth, the Shamrock boy eliminated any hope of catching his opponent from the border city. His ball missed the green, settling deep in the tall grass surrounding the green. He turned to Joe and finally uttered his first words to him. "That was a hell of a shot, Joe! You're playing well. I can't believe you're doing it with those fucked-up clubs!"

Joe was surprised to hear that, as one normally compliments a good shot immediately following it, but he appreciated the comment anyway. He smiled at the Shamrock boy and said, "Thanks." They then walked to the green in the steadily flowing rain. There was not a single dry part of their bodies, but that seemed to matter little now. They were almost done. They finished the seventeenth hole, and the group headed to the eighteenth tee box.

The Shamrock player, who was clearly down to his Mustang opponent, felt no qualms about trying to reach for the green in two, no matter the rain. He swung with all his might after Joe had already positioned his ball on the fairway, but this time he pushed it solidly to the right and slammed against an overhanging branch of a tree. The boy didn't care about his round anymore so there was no need for him to express his dissatisfaction. By the time they reached the green, the crowd was waiting for the players, who were walking closely together, exchanging comments that caused each to laugh, as though they were playing a casual round back home.

J. B. and his associates turned to each other with a puzzled look. They failed to understand why the young golfers did not appreciate the tension of the event. They quietly chose to see that as a good sign.

When the boys finished the hole, they shook hands and spoke briefly by the flag, but J. B. and the others could not hear what they said. Joe walked over to them with a smile and showed J. B. his scorecard.

J. B. studied it carefully and then handed it back to Joe. "Make sure you sign it and turn it in, son."

"Yessir," Joe replied as he took the card and headed to the scoring tent.

"He shot a seventy-seven!" J. B. reported to Hiram and Joe Mitchell.

"Wow!" the two exclaimed with eyes wide open.

"I don't think I coulda broken eighty in these conditions," Joe Mitchell stated.

"Hey, look," Hiram said to the others. "Here comes Mario and his group."

They noticed Mario was walking around looking at the ground a short distance from the green. He was looking for a distance marker before he determined what club to hit. He paused for a moment upon finding one and stood there looking at the flag, then the marker, and then the ball. He then pulled an eight-iron from his bag and took his swing. The ball flew up and headed for the flag but hit short of the green, stopping on the frog hair about twenty feet from the pin.

"That's puttable," observed Joe Mitchell.

"He's made those before, Coach," asserted young Joe, who had returned to the green after turning in his score. "He's made many of those on me before!"

Mario made his way onto the green and saw where the ball had stopped. He had started to pull out his wedge when he looked at Joe, who shook his head in disapproval. Mario smiled and then put the wedge back and pulled out his putter. Joe returned the smile. When it was his turn, Mario positioned himself next to his ball and confidently made his stroke. Though he did not succeed in holing out for birdie, the putt for par pleased everyone who witnessed it, prompting generous applause.

J. B. waited anxiously for Mario to walk over to report his score.

"What did the Shamrock kid shoot?" he asked after writing Mario's score down.

"He totally fell apart, Coach. It was sad to see!"

"What did he shoot?" J. B. repeated.

"Oh. A ninety-two," Mario said.

J. B. looked at Hiram, his eyes now revealing his emotions.

"Don't say it, J. B.!" Hiram warned. "We've gotta wait for Felipe and Gene."

J. B. nodded in agreement but said nothing.

Mario then stood by Joe and asked, "Did you kick his butt again for me?"

"You better believe it!" Joe answered with glee in his voice. "Now you really owe me!"

"Thanks, but you'll have to wait to get back home to collect."

"What? Joe asked.

"I don't know, but I'll think of sumpin."

Everyone was now waiting anxiously for Felipe. His score would give the greatest indication of where they stood against Shamrock. Ranger would not be repeating, but Shamrock could not be ruled out.

"There's Felipe!" Mario informed the rest when he noticed Felipe's group approach the green.

The rain, though steady, had not produced any thunder or lightning, so J. B. privately thought there was now a chance that the round would not be canceled short of completion. He just needed for Felipe and Gene to finish and rule that option out.

Felipe came to the eighteenth green seeking a par to cap off an admirable round, considering the elements. Before he could complete his round, though, he waited for the other players to hole out. He finalized his round with that par and walked over to his teammates and J. B. He showed them his card and headed toward the scoring tent with a smile on his face.

"Can you believe that?" J. B. asked rhetorically. "He shot the same score as yesterday!"

"A seventy-nine? " Joe Mitchell asked, even though he knew the answer.

"That's amazing!" Hiram exclaimed. "In this weather?"

It would now be up to Gene to determine whether their quest for the gold would materialize or whether they would fall short again.

After what seemed like an eternity to J. B. and the others, Gene and his group finally appeared about 150 yards away from the flag. When the rest had hit their shots, Gene took dead aim at the flag. With the nerves of an older player, Gene took a healthy swing at the ball, producing a high flight. Everyone witnessing the shot was immediately convinced that it was going to hit the flag, as it was tracking right at it. It must have waved good-bye to the hole, as it continued flying past it and landed in the sand bunker situated on the far side of the green.

"Ahh" were the sighs of the fan as they expressed their disappointment that the result did not match the perfect strike. Joe, Felipe, and Mario hurried over to take a look at the ball in the bunker. It was not a bad lie, but the sand soaked by the rain would prove quite challenging. The boys looked at each other and grimaced. When Gene walked over to see his ball, Joe and the others pulled him aside.

"Gene, I don't want to scare you, but you need to get up and down for us!" Joe admonished.

"Yeah, you need to make par!" Mario and Felipe chimed in.

"Why?" Gene asked, now getting anxious.

"If you par the hole, we win," Joe stated quite firmly. "But if you don't, we lose!" Mario warned.

"Yeah!" Felipe added. "You gotta make a par!"

"Do it for San Fe, Gene!" Joe insisted.

Gene bit his lip and looked at his ball lying on the wet sand, lamenting in his mind that he should have hit a nine-iron instead. His decision had placed his team in jeopardy of losing the championship. "All right! I can do this!" he asserted to his teammates.

"Yeah. You can do this, Gene!" Joe confirmed.

"Do it, Gene!" Mario ordered. "For San Fe!"

Gene looked at the flag and then his ball again. He pulled his sand wedge from his wet canvas bag and walked into the bunker. The grip on the club was also wet, so he told himself to grip down harder so that the clubhead wouldn't twist as it hit the sand. As he was about to hit the ball, J. B., Hiram, Joe Mitchell, and the other boys held their breath.

Gene glanced one more time at the flag and then began his swing. "Splat" was the sound they all heard as the club hit the wet sand behind the ball. A clump of caked-up sand flew up along with the ball.

Everyone waited in anticipation to see where the ball would land, and it seemed like it took forever for it to get there. The sand landed first about 10 yards onto the green, followed by the ball. It connected with the wet grass of the green and started to roll toward the hole. "That's a good line," they all thought. Gene stared at the ball as it rolled and rolled closer to the hole, deciding to stop one foot short of the cup.

"Yes!" Gene shouted as he slammed his fist against the air, signaling to all that he had pulled it off.

Deafening cheers and shouts of "great shot" from the observant crowd immediately followed.

"You did it, Gene!" yelled Joe as Gene tried to collect himself before attempting his putt. He would have to complement his great sand shot with the putt to seal his par. The players asked him if he wanted to putt it out, but Gene saw some wet sand stuck to his ball and indicated that he preferred to wait so he could clean it. The other players then proceeded to finish their rounds, giving Gene his chance at par.

He had only parred two other holes, but this would be the crucial one. He placed his ball down and forced himself to stay calm. He did not want to lose the prize on such an easy putt. He stuck to his routine by carefully looking at the short line to the hole and then set up to hit it. As soon as he struck it, he closed his eyes and waited for that sound. "Clup, clup," he heard, and he knew that he had accomplished what his teammates had asked him to do.

The boys then rushed over to greet him. "You did it, Gene! You won it for us!"

"I did?" Gene asked. "Yes! I did!" he exclaimed with joy as the boys hugged him and patted him on the back.

J. B., Hiram, and Joe Mitchell quickly joined them, but they couldn't understand why the boys had made so much fuss. After writing down Gene's score and that of the Shamrock and Ranger boys, J. B. directed everyone to the official scoreboard. They all gathered as they patiently waited for the officials to post the scores. They knew that they had won, but they had to wait for the official results before they could begin to celebrate.

The main official called out the scores as the local pro wrote them down on the board. The total for Ranger, the last year's champion, was posted. It was a 691. Then Shamrock's score was posted. A 678. The official then called out San Felipe's total. A 643.

Gene stared at it for a moment and quickly did the math in his head. "Wait a minute! You guys told me that I needed to make my par to win! Hell, we won by thirty-five strokes!" he shouted as he slapped Mario on the arm.

The boys then began laughing as they grabbed Gene and started tickling him in the ribs.

"We gotcha!" Mario shouted amid the laughter of his teammates.

"You guys scared the shit out of me!" Gene claimed. "I can't believe you did that to me!"

"We were just trying to make sure you proved you could do it!" Joe explained as the laughter continued.

J. B. embraced Hiram and then Joe Mitchell before he walked over to the boys to congratulate them. It was a truly happy gathering as they waited next for the presentation of the trophy and the medals.

Not only had San Felipe won, but Joe captured the individual medalist with a total score of 150. Felipe took the silver medal with a score of 158, and Mario claimed the bronze with a score of 159. A clean sweep for the Mustangs.

As they waited for the usual trophy presentation ceremony, an official of the TIL walked over to J. B. and pulled him aside. He had a large shiny trophy with a plaque that read "1957 Class A State Boys' Golf Champions" and a big manila envelope, which he handed to J. B.

"Here's your trophy and your medals, Coach," he said with no explanation or congratulations. J. B. was puzzled, as were Hiram and Joe Mitchell.

"Wait a minute," Joe Mitchell said. "Isn't there some type of presentation ceremony at these things?"

The official looked at Joe Mitchell and J. B. and appeared to have trouble coming up with an answer. "Well, the weather's not gonna let us do that this year," he said and walked away.

Though they were ecstatic knowing they had won the state championship, every one of the boys and the adults had an empty feeling inside but couldn't articulate it. Receiving the prizes in this manner felt anticlimactic.

"What's going on, Coach?" Mario asked.

J. B. looked at Hiram and Joe Mitchell and then said, "Nothing, boys. Looks like we'll have to have our own ceremony! Let's go home!"

The boys then grabbed their luxurious bags and clubs and put them away in the trunk of J. B.'s car and drove away.

On the outskirts of town, J. B. stopped to get gas, but he also made a telephone call to someone. He said nothing to the rest when he climbed back into the car and headed for home.

Though they had been victorious and should have been noisily expressing joy, a general feeling of emptiness permeated the car, and no one said a word. Something made them feel as though they had been cheated out of that joy. After traveling for about an hour, Hiram broke the silence when he said, "I bet you boys are hungry."

"Yessir!" the boys quickly replied.

"Well, J. B., don't you think the boys deserve a good steak?" Hiram continued.

"Yes, they do, indeed!" J. B. responded.

"What's a steak, Coach?" Gene asked rather innocently.

"You boys never had a steak before?" Hiram asked in amazement. "No, sir, Mr. Valdes," Joe confirmed.

"No sir," the other boys agreed.

"Okay, then. We're going to stop at Mike's Place in San Antonio and get us a nice, juicy steak! You okay with that, J. B.?" Hiram inquired.

"Sounds fine to me!" J. B. said. "What about you boys?" he asked as he peered at them through the rearview mirror.

The boys looked at each other, nodded their heads up and down, and then Joe exclaimed, "Yes, we deserve a good steak!"

"But I still wanna know what a steak is!" Gene cried out.

They all started to laugh as they drove into downtown San Antonio with Hiram explaining that a steak was a cut of meat from a cow and how it would be cooked to taste its best.

When they arrived at Mike's Place, the group was seated at a table in the middle of the room. All around them were people sitting at tables talking and enjoying their meals and drinks. The boys noticed that the patrons were either fellow Mexicans or African Americans, with not a single Anglo in the room, except for Joe Mitchell. "How weird!" they all thought to themselves, not catching on to the irony.

When the meals were finally brought and set down on the table in front of each of them, the boys looked closely at the sizzling pieces of meat at the center of their plates but waited for a moment before touching anything. Hiram noticed that none had started eating, and he instinctively knew that an explanation was necessary. "Use the fork with one hand and the knife with the other to cut your steak into small pieces to eat it," he instructed as he demonstrated with the one on his plate. The boys looked at him intently and then grabbed their utensils and attempted to imitate Hiram.

Felipe was having a particularly difficult time with his task. As he struggled to slide the knife against an edge of his steak while holding the fork with his left hand, the grip on his fork slipped right at the moment that he pushed the knife away from him. Suddenly the steak slid off the plate and flew right by J. B. and onto the floor. Laughter quickly broke out among those at his table and then spread among the other patrons when they noticed what had just happened.

J. B. bent over to the floor and picked up the steak and placed it back on Felipe's plate. "That's all right, Phil. I'll have the waitress bring you another one." He consoled him as the other boys were still laughing.

"Guess you shoulda used a Vardon grip on that fork," Mario facetiously observed. The laughter increased, but Felipe now joined in, as he found the incident funny even though it was at his expense.

It proved to be quite an enjoyable day, as it was capped off with a meal befitting champions.

CHAPTER TWENTY

T HE FOLLOWING MONDAY MORNING seemed like every typical day in high school when the boys returned to San Felipe. Few people had been told what they had accomplished the week before, but a few friends who already knew congratulated them on their feat. After roll call, each of the teachers received a note to lead their classes directly to the auditorium. The assistant principal was assigned to pull each of the boys from his class, but they were taken to the principal's office and told to wait there until they were called.

As soon as the classrooms were empty and the entire campus was gathered in the auditorium, the assistant principal led the boys backstage and told them to wait. There was silence for a while and then they heard J. B.'s voice through the loudspeakers.

"Good morning, everybody. Many of you don't know that I had the privilege of spending four days with some of the best kids I have had the pleasure of knowing. I want to tell you all that I would be proud of calling any of them my son," J. B. said as his voice began to crack with emotion. "I also had the honor of witnessing an amazing event in Austin. No, I dare say I witnessed a miracle that really touched my heart and those of all who supported the idea of putting a golf team together to represent all of you Mustangs! Students and teachers, I proudly present to you, the 1957 Class A State Golf Champions! Come on out here, boys!"

Cheers erupted as the boys came out from behind the curtain, and the Mustang band started playing the school fight song. The boys walked over to J. B., waving their hands to the students who were now standing up clapping and whistling in admiration as J. B. handed the boys their trophy. The boys were totally surprised, but they now began to feel what they should have felt in Austin following their victory. That they truly were the champions now started to sink in.

Once the yelling and clapping subsided, J. B. continued with his presentations. "I also want to let you know that not only did they win as a team by thirty-five strokes …" The cheers and whistling resumed, and J. B. waited for the sounds to calm down. "But we took all of the individual titles as well. The bronze medal for third was won by Mario Lomas. Come here, Mario!" J. B. called to him and handed him the bronze medal.

"Thank you, Coach!" Mario politely said as he grabbed the medal and placed it around his neck. He waved to the students as the cheers resumed.

J. B. continued, "The silver medal for second place was won by Felipe Romero! Come here, Felipe."

Felipe smiled and walked over to J. B. as the crowd cheered on. He then placed his silver medal around his neck and kissed it.

"And the gold medal for the individual champion goes to Joe Trevino!" J. B. now was shouting into the microphone as the students had begun to truly realize what the boys had accomplished. "Now this trophy," he said, pointing at the shiny prize on the podium, "will be displayed in the school's trophy case, but the boys will be getting their own championship medal."

"Wait, Coach!" Mario urged.

"Yeah, wait, Coach!" the boys pleaded in unison and then whispered something to J. B.

After hearing what the boys told him, he said, "I agree." He returned to the microphone and stated, "We do have one member of the team who was not able to travel and compete with the team in Austin, but the boys and I feel he also deserves to get his own medal. Lupe Felan. Come up here, Lupe!"

The students around Lupe started patting him on the back and coaxing him to go up on stage. He did so reluctantly but then rushed from his seat and to the stairs when he heard the team members yell out his name to the cheers and applause of all those present. He was greeted by the boys, and J. B. handed him a medal, which he accepted with tears in his eyes and looked over at the boys.

"You are one of us!" Gene told him.

"Yeah, you're a champion too, Lupe!" Mario added. "Yeah!" Joe and Felipe agreed.

When the cheers and whistling had calmed down, J. B. had other announcements. "Now what we're going to do is assemble outside and along Garza Street in front of the school. The band will lead us out to begin our parade, and then school will be out for the rest of the day!" With that the students broke out in even louder cheers and began filing outside.

J. B. gathered the five boys and led them to a convertible that had been parked outside. Apparently J. B. had arranged to borrow the car from one of his friends, and the cheerleaders had decorated it with purple and gold streamers and a sign that said "1957 State Golf Champions." Hiram and Joe Mitchell were waiting for the boys in the front seat as they each climbed in and sat on the backrest of the backseat as instructed. The band then began to march south on Garza Street, the main drag of San Felipe, and the car with the boys followed.

Unbeknownst to the boys, J. B. had informed several people to go to each house on Garza Street and ask the residents to go outside their houses and get ready to cheer at the appointed time. They did as asked and lined the entire street, where they were clapping and cheering as the boys rode slowly by. The boys waved back at the crowd, which was cheering in celebration of their Mustang miracle.

Left to right: J.B. Pena, Joe Trevino, Mario Lomas, Gene
Vasquez, Felipe Romero, Lupe Felan and Hiram Valdes

Left to right: Mario Lomas, Joe Trevino, Lupe Felan, Felipe Romero and J. B. Pena

POSTWORD

Since the book was originally published I have been asked by many readers what happened to the golfers in the years that followed the championship. At their suggestion, I have decided to include in this postword a brief summary of their lives after the championship.

JOE TREVINO

The winner of the gold medal for his individual championship, Joe was highly recruited by every Southwest Conference School for their golf teams. However, being a humble and modest small town boy, Joe decided to stay in Del Rio. After graduation he began working in several jobs before ending at the Laughlin Air Force Base Golf Course working in their maintenance division. He quickly learned golf course agronomics and was called upon by the course managers to help with the problems they encountered in keeping the course green. The Base Commander at the time would often ask Joe to play with him in matches against other officers and most of the time Joe and the Commander would win because of Joe's play. When the Commander was transferred to a Southern California base, he asked Joe to transfer with him. Joe agreed and soon found himself in California tending to the Air Force golf courses in the area. In his spare time, Joe would compete in local and regional tournaments with regular success. After over 34 years of Civil Service employment, Joe retired and returned to Del Rio where he now lives. He still plays golf regularly with other members of the team.

FELIPE ROMERO

The winner of the silver medal, Felipe Romero, was the only one who played golf professionally after graduating from San Felipe High School. He attended the first national PGA Business School in San Antonio, Texas and learned the business side of golf. During the 1960's, 70's and 80's, he competed professionally in national and international golf mini tours. He worked as a bus conductor and instructor for the Metropolitan Transit Authority in Houston, Texas for 29 years before retiring.

He was married to the late Oralia Delgado Romero with whom he had three children. He has seven grandchildren and three great-grandchildren. He continues to enjoy playing the game of golf today.

MARIO LOMAS

After graduating from San Felipe High School in 1959, the bronze medal winner, Mario Reyes Lomas, went to work as a professional caddy in the PGA Tour for many years, caddying for such golf stars as George Archer and others. He was forced to discontinue his caddying days when he hurt his knee in a terrible automobile accident. He now works for a golf club in Abilene, Texas and continues to play the game of golf which he credits with having saved his life as a youth.

HIGINIO "GENE" VASQUEZ

After graduating from San Felipe High School, Gene enrolled in Sul Ross College (now known as Sul Ross State University) and graduated in 1965 with a Bachelor of Arts Degree in Education. He then went to work for the San Felipe Independent School District as a teacher and taught for over ten years. In 1971 he became involved in the real estate business in which he continues working today.

Gene is the father of seven children, Gene, David, Leo, Denise, Laura, Lorena, and Miguel Angel Vasquez. He lives in Del Rio and still enjoys the game of golf, along with fishing and playing the slots at the casino.

He credits the game of golf as having provided a very positive impact on his life and through which he has met many positive minded people.

GUADALUPE "LUPE" FELAN

After graduating from San Felipe High School in 1957, Lupe enlisted in the United States Marine Corps and served his country for over thirty years before retiring in 1990. During his years in the Marine Corps he participated in golf competitions in the military.

After retiring from the marines, Mr. Felan went to work for the State of California, Department of Motor Vehicles from which he has now retired.

Mr. Felan continues to play golf as an active member of the South California Golf Association, The Southern California Mexican American Golf Association and the Marine Combat Center Golf Association and has maintained a single digit handicap. He presently lives with his wife in Yucca Valley, California.

J.B. PENA

Mr. Pena continued to work as superintendent of the San Felipe Independent School District until 1967. He then became Curriculum Director for the San Felipe I.S.D. and then Bilingual Education Director for San Felipe I.S.D. and the newly created San Felipe Del Rio Consolidated School District until his retirement in 1979. He coached the golf team for several more years after the Championship before turning the reigns over to another teacher of the school district. After retiring, he spent many years devoting his efforts to local civic activities and charities including those sponsored by the San Felipe Lions Club. He played golf more regularly and I have the honor to report that I played golf with him and Hiram Valdes beginning in 1979 and continuing until I left Del Rio in 1985. Sadly, Mr. Pena died in 1986.

HIRAM VALDES

Mr. Valdes spent his career with Civil Service, working primarily as an aircraft mechanic at Laughlin Air Force Base in Del Rio, retiring after 32 years. Long after the team won the 1957 State Golf Championship, he continued playing the game he loved and was a regular at San Felipe Country Club which eventually admitted nonwhites as members. Unfortunately he was not able to witness the accolades given to the team as he died in 2007 at the age of 93. The team dedicated a bench in his honor which is situated on the grounds of the San Felipe Country Club.

Since this book first came out, the team has received widespread publicity and recognition. Their story has been covered by several newspapers and magazines. In March of 2011 they were recognized and honored by the Texas House of Representatives for their achievement 54 years after the fact. Under the sponsorship of Representative Pete Gallego from Alpine, Texas, the House unanimously passed a resolution honoring each of the members as well as J.B. Pena and Hiram Valdes.

In January of 2012 they were inducted into the Latino International Sports Hall of Fame in a moving ceremony in Laredo, Texas joining such other sports stars as Jorge Posada of the New York Yankees and Jaime Garcia of the World Series Champion St. Louis Cardinals.

In July of 2012, George Lopez announced that through his production company, Travieso Productions, a movie about the team and their accomplishment would be made.

Many thanks go out to all who have supported this book and have spread the story of the Mustang Miracle.

Left to right: Mario Lomas, Gene Vasquez, Felipe Romero, Nancy Rodriguez (Hiram Valdes' daughter), me, Laura Pena Gamez (JB Pena's daughter), Lupe Felan, and seated Joe Trevino.

Left to right: Lupe Felan, Felipe Romero, Mario Lomas, Gene Vasquez and Humberto Garcia. By microphone is the Speaker Pro tem.

Left to right: Joe Trevino, Felipe Romero, Mario Lomas, State
Rep. Pete Gallego, me, Lupe Felan and Gene Vasquez.

Left to right: Andy Ramos, Hall of Fame Chairman, Joe Trevino, Ignacio Urrabazo,
President of International Bank of Commerce and San Felipe Alumni, Mario Lomas,
Person in green Blazer unknown, Lupe Felan, Gene Vasquez and Felipe Romero.

STATE CHAMPS

MARIO LOMAS – 3rd place State
   Medalist – 36
FELIPE ROMERO – 2nd place State
   Medalist – 38
HIGINIO VASQUEZ – 15
COACH J. B. PENA – 16
LUPE FELAN – 10
JOE TREVINO – State Medalist – 26

About the Author

 Humberto G. Garcia was born and raised in the San Felipe area of the City of Del Rio. He attended the schools in the San Felipe Independent School District and would have graduated from San Felipe High School in 1972 but for the consolidation of the district with the Del Rio Independent School District by a federal court order in the summer of 1971. In fact, his witnessing of the events in the U. S. District Court for the Eastern District of Texas involving the battle between the San Felipe and Del Rio school officials served as a factor in his seeking of a legal education. Following graduation from high school, he attended the University of Texas at Austin where he received his Bachelor of Arts in Government in 1975. He then attended the University of Texas, School of Law and received his Doctorate of Jurisprudence in 1978. While in law school, he developed a strong interest in golf, having been introduced to the game by two of his study partners. He is quite familiar with golf as he has competed in several professional tournaments and continues to do so today. While as an undergraduate he took several courses in Mexican-American studies where he learned the history of the treatment of his ethnic group by American society. He also experienced firsthand discrimination and unfair treatment while growing up as a migrant farm worker with his family. His tripartite knowledge of the subjects covered in this book gives him a unique perspective into the experience of the San Felipe High School 1957 Golf Team. It is with the clear understanding of this experience that he is able to describe the significance of a bright moment in American history for a people who were otherwise deprived of an equal opportunity.